The Untold History of Everyday Objects

Shah Rukh

Published by Shah Rukh, 2024.

While every precaution has been taken in the preparation of this book, the publisher assumes no responsibility for errors or omissions, or for damages resulting from the use of the information contained herein.

THE UNTOLD HISTORY OF EVERYDAY OBJECTS

First edition. June 25, 2024.

Written by Shah Rukh.

Table of Contents

Prologue

Every day, we interact with hundreds of objects without giving them a second thought. From the toothbrush we use each morning to the light switch we flick off at night, these items are integral to our daily routines. Yet, behind each of these seemingly mundane objects lies a rich tapestry of history, innovation, and human ingenuity.

"The Untold History of Everyday Objects" seeks to unravel the stories behind the common items that populate our lives. This book will take you on a journey through time, exploring the evolution of different objects that have, in their own unique ways, shaped our world.

Consider the humble paperclip. It's a small, unassuming piece of metal that holds our documents together. But did you know it was invented over a century ago and became a symbol of resistance during World War II? Or the safety pin, which not only revolutionized fasteners but also played a role in ancient Rome's fashion?

Each chapter in this book will delve into the origin stories of these objects, revealing the challenges and triumphs faced by their inventors. You'll discover how a simple idea, often born out of necessity, can transform into an indispensable tool used by millions. From the sticky note that started as a failed adhesive experiment to the zipper that revolutionized clothing, these stories are a testament to human creativity and perseverance.

As you read, you'll gain a newfound appreciation for the items that surround you. You'll learn how the coffee mug you hold every morning is part of a long tradition of beverage containers that dates back to ancient civilizations. You'll see how the development of the electric fan helped modernize homes and workplaces, making our environments more comfortable and productive.

This book is not just about the objects themselves, but also about the people behind them. It's about the inventors who dared to think differently, the engineers who brought ideas to life, and the everyday users who adopted these innovations and made them part of their daily lives. Their stories are interwoven with the history of the objects they created, providing a rich and engaging narrative that brings these everyday items to life.

So, as you embark on this journey through "The Untold History of Everyday Objects," prepare to see the world around you with fresh eyes. The next time you clip a stack of papers, zip up your jacket, or jot down a note, you'll remember that even the simplest object has a story worth telling. Welcome to the fascinating world of everyday objects—stories of ingenuity, creativity, and the relentless pursuit of making life a little bit easier.

Chapter 1: The Evolution of the Toothbrush

The story of the toothbrush is a fascinating journey that spans thousands of years and traverses numerous cultures, reflecting the evolution of human hygiene practices and advancements in material science. The earliest forms of toothbrushes can be traced back to ancient civilizations, long before the invention of modern dentistry. These primitive tools, though rudimentary, laid the groundwork for the sophisticated devices we use today to maintain oral health.

In ancient times, the concept of dental care was rudimentary and varied greatly across different cultures. One of the earliest known toothbrush-like tools dates back to around 3500-3000 BCE in ancient Mesopotamia and Egypt. These early tools were essentially "chew sticks," which were twigs or small branches with frayed ends that could be used to scrub the teeth. The Egyptians, in particular, are noted for their contributions to early dental care. They would use sticks from aromatic trees to clean their teeth, as well as tooth powders made from a mixture of ashes, ox hooves, eggshells, and pumice. These powders, while crude by today's standards, were an early attempt to combat dental decay and freshen breath.

As we move forward in history, we find that different cultures developed their own methods for maintaining oral hygiene. In ancient India, around 1600 BCE, the practice of using neem tree twigs, known as "datun," was widespread. Neem twigs were chosen for their antiseptic properties, and this practice is still in use in some parts of India today. Meanwhile, in China, around 1498, a significant advancement in toothbrush technology was made. The Chinese are credited with creating the first bristle toothbrush, which was made from hog bristles attached to a bamboo or bone handle. This design was notably more effective than the chew sticks as it could better reach and clean between teeth.

The Chinese toothbrush design gradually spread to Europe through trade and cultural exchange, particularly during the Ming Dynasty. However, in Europe, toothbrushes did not become popular until the 17th century. Before then, Europeans primarily used a cloth or sponge to clean their teeth, often combined with abrasive powders made from substances like chalk, salt, or brick dust. These methods, while somewhat effective at removing surface stains, were harsh on the enamel and could lead to tooth damage.

The 18th century marked a significant turning point in the history of the toothbrush with the invention of the first mass-produced toothbrush in England. In 1780, William Addis, an Englishman, is credited with creating a prototype of the modern toothbrush. According to legend, Addis conceived the idea while in prison, where he noticed that using a rag with soot and salt to clean his teeth was ineffective. He fashioned a brush by drilling small holes into a bone and inserting tufts of boar bristles, secured with glue. This design proved to be much more effective and laid the foundation for the toothbrushes we are familiar with today.

Following the introduction of Addis's toothbrush, the 19th century saw significant advancements in toothbrush design and materials. With the advent of the Industrial Revolution, toothbrushes became more accessible and affordable due to improved manufacturing techniques. Bone handles and natural bristles were standard, but the bristles often came from animals such as pigs or horses, which could be harsh and uncomfortable. The invention of synthetic materials in the 20th century revolutionized the toothbrush once again. In 1938, nylon was introduced by the DuPont company, leading to the creation of the first toothbrush with synthetic bristles, known as Doctor West's Miracle Toothbrush. Nylon bristles were more hygienic and durable than animal hair, and they did not retain bacteria or absorb water, making them an ideal choice for dental care.

The mid-20th century also saw the rise of the electric toothbrush. The first modern electric toothbrush, the Broxodent, was developed in Switzerland in 1954 by Dr. Philippe-Guy Woog. It was initially designed for patients with limited motor skills, such as those with disabilities or the elderly. The electric toothbrush offered a significant improvement in cleaning efficiency and became increasingly popular over the following decades. Today, electric toothbrushes have advanced considerably, featuring rechargeable batteries, oscillating and vibrating heads, and even smart technology that connects to mobile apps to monitor brushing habits.

The late 20th and early 21st centuries have seen continual innovation in toothbrush design and technology. Manufacturers have introduced a variety of bristle shapes, sizes, and stiffness levels to cater to different dental needs. Some toothbrushes now feature angled or multi-level bristles designed to reach more areas of the mouth and remove plaque more effectively. Additionally, the handles of toothbrushes have been ergonomically designed to provide a better grip and ensure more effective brushing techniques.

Modern toothbrushes are often made from a combination of plastic materials, including polypropylene and polyethylene, which are durable, lightweight, and cost-effective. Environmental concerns have also driven innovation in toothbrush materials, with the introduction of biodegradable and eco-friendly options made from bamboo and other sustainable materials. These alternatives aim to reduce the environmental impact of plastic toothbrushes, which contribute to landfill waste and ocean pollution.

In recent years, there has been a growing emphasis on the integration of technology into toothbrushes to enhance oral health care. Smart toothbrushes equipped with sensors and Bluetooth connectivity can track brushing habits, provide feedback on brushing techniques, and even detect early signs of dental issues. Some models include features such as timers to ensure the recommended brushing duration and pressure sensors to prevent over-brushing, which can damage gums and enamel.

The evolution of the toothbrush reflects broader changes in society's approach to health and hygiene. From ancient chew sticks to high-tech smart toothbrushes, the quest for effective dental care has driven continuous innovation and improvement.

Chapter 2: The Surprising Origins of the Safety Pin

The safety pin, an everyday object taken for granted by most, has a rich and intricate history that stretches back millennia, revealing fascinating insights into human ingenuity and the evolution of fashion and functionality.

The origins of the safety pin can be traced back to ancient times, long before the birth of modern civilization. The earliest known predecessors of the safety pin were found in Europe and the Middle East, dating back to the Bronze Age, around 3000 to 1000 BCE. These early fasteners, known as "fibulae," were used by ancient peoples to secure clothing. The fibulae were typically made from metal such as bronze or iron, and their design varied widely, reflecting the craftsmanship and aesthetic preferences of different cultures.

The fibulae served not only as functional fasteners but also as decorative items, often intricately designed and adorned with carvings, gemstones, and precious metals. They were used to fasten garments like cloaks and tunics, which were essential for protection against the elements. The design of the fibulae evolved over time, with different regions developing distinct styles. For instance, the ancient Greeks and Romans used fibulae with elaborate shapes and designs, often featuring intricate filigree work and depictions of animals or mythological figures. The functional aspect of the fibula, which included a pin, a spring mechanism, and a catch plate, bears a striking resemblance to the modern safety pin, illustrating the enduring utility of this ancient invention.

The evolution of the fibula continued through the centuries, and by the time of the Roman Empire, it had become a common and essential item in everyday life. Roman soldiers used fibulae to fasten their cloaks, while civilians used them to secure their garments and display their social status. The designs varied from simple and utilitarian to highly ornate and symbolic. Some fibulae were designed to be worn as brooches, highlighting their dual function as both a fastening device and a piece of jewelry.

As we move forward in history, the use of fibulae and similar fasteners spread throughout Europe, the Middle East, and Asia, reflecting the interconnectedness of ancient civilizations through trade and cultural exchange. In medieval Europe, for example, fibulae were replaced by more elaborate brooches and clasps, which were used to fasten clothing and also served as symbols of status and wealth. These medieval fasteners were often made from precious metals and adorned with gemstones, and their designs reflected the artistic styles and cultural influences of the time.

Despite the widespread use of various fasteners throughout history, the specific design and function of the modern safety pin remained undeveloped until the 19th century. It was during this period that the Industrial Revolution brought about significant advancements in manufacturing and material science, paving the way for new inventions and improvements in everyday objects. The safety pin, as we know it today, was invented in 1849 by Walter Hunt, an American mechanic and prolific inventor. Hunt's version of the safety pin was not only practical but also ingeniously designed to include a clasp that covered the sharp point, making it safe to use.

Walter Hunt's invention of the safety pin was driven by a pressing need to pay off a debt of $15. In just a few hours, Hunt conceptualized and created a prototype for a pin with a spring mechanism and a clasp. He sold the rights to his invention for $400, a sum that may seem modest today but was a significant amount at the time. Hunt's safety pin consisted of a single piece of wire coiled into a spring at one end, which provided tension, and a clasp at the other end to secure the pin in place and cover the sharp point. This simple yet effective design allowed the safety pin to be used safely and easily, making it a revolutionary tool for fastening fabrics and other materials.

The introduction of the safety pin had a profound impact on everyday life, offering a convenient and reliable solution for fastening clothing, securing bandages, and performing a multitude of other tasks. It quickly became an indispensable item in households around the world. The safety pin's design also made it easy to mass-produce, which helped to drive down costs and make it widely accessible to people of all social classes.

The safety pin's utility extended beyond mere fastening, as it became a symbol of practicality and ingenuity. During the American Civil War, soldiers used safety pins to mend their uniforms and secure bandages, underscoring the pin's versatility and importance in everyday life. The safety pin also played a crucial role in the suffrage movement of the early 20th century. Women suffragists used safety pins to attach their banners and sashes, which they wore during marches and rallies to advocate for women's right to vote. The safety pin thus became associated with the struggle for social and political change, highlighting its symbolic significance in addition to its practical uses.

In addition to its practical applications, the safety pin also became a staple in fashion and popular culture. During the punk rock movement of the 1970s and 1980s, safety pins were used as a form of rebellion and self-expression. Punk rockers would wear safety pins as accessories, often attaching them to their clothing, piercing their skin, and using them to create unique and unconventional styles. The safety pin became a symbol of the punk movement's rejection of mainstream culture and its embrace of a DIY ethos.

The safety pin's influence extended into the realm of high fashion as well. Designers such as Vivienne Westwood and Jean-Paul Gaultier incorporated safety pins into their clothing and accessories, transforming a humble tool into a statement piece that challenged traditional notions of fashion and beauty. The safety pin's journey from a practical fastener to a fashion icon highlights its versatility and enduring appeal.

Chapter 3: The History of the Paperclip

The paperclip, a ubiquitous item found in offices, homes, and classrooms around the world, is an unassuming yet remarkably ingenious invention. Its history spans more than a century and reflects a fascinating evolution in the fields of office supplies, manufacturing, and design. The journey of the paperclip from its early beginnings to its current form reveals much about the development of modern society and the ingenious ways in which simple problems have been solved with elegant, functional solutions.

The concept of the paperclip can be traced back to ancient times, when various methods were used to bind papers and documents together. In the medieval period, people used wax seals, ribbons, and cords to keep their important documents in order. In some cases, pins were used to attach papers to boards or other surfaces, ensuring that they would stay in place. These early methods, while effective to a certain extent, lacked the simplicity and convenience of the modern paperclip.

The true story of the paperclip begins in the 19th century, a period marked by rapid industrialization and the proliferation of paper products. As more businesses, organizations, and individuals began to rely on paper for communication, record-keeping, and administration, the need for efficient and effective methods of organizing documents became increasingly apparent. It was during this time that the paperclip as we know it began to take shape.

The earliest attempts to create a paperclip involved a variety of designs and materials. In 1835, Samuel B. Fay of the United States was granted a patent for a device designed to attach tickets to fabrics, which could also be used to hold papers together. Fay's design featured a U-shaped pin with an extended arm that could be inserted into a fabric or paper, effectively securing it in place. This invention, while not yet a paperclip in the modern sense, demonstrated the growing interest in devices for fastening papers.

Another notable early design came in 1842 when John Ireland Howe, an American doctor and inventor, created a machine that produced straight pins. While Howe's invention was initially intended for the textile industry, straight pins quickly found a new use in the office environment as a means of temporarily binding papers. The use of pins to hold papers together, however, had its drawbacks, including the risk of puncturing or damaging the documents.

The quest for a better solution continued throughout the 19th century, leading to a series of inventive designs that brought us closer to the modern paperclip. In 1867, Samuel Slocum, another American inventor, patented a novel device for fastening papers. Slocum's invention featured a twisted piece of metal wire that could be wrapped around a stack of papers, securing them together without the need for perforation. While this design was an improvement over straight pins, it was still not as convenient or reliable as the paperclip would become.

The turning point in the history of the paperclip came in 1899 when Johan Vaaler, a Norwegian inventor, created a design that closely resembled the paperclips we use today. Vaaler's invention featured a simple, efficient design consisting of a single piece of wire bent into a loop with two ends that could be slipped over a stack of papers to hold them together. Although Vaaler's paperclip was patented in Germany and the United States, it was not immediately successful due to a lack of effective manufacturing methods and the competition from other fastening devices.

Around the same time that Vaaler was working on his design, another significant development occurred in the United States. The Gem Manufacturing Company of England introduced a paperclip with a double oval shape that would become the standard design for paperclips worldwide. The Gem paperclip, as it came to be known, featured a simple yet highly effective design that used a single loop of wire to create two layers of tension, allowing it to securely hold a stack of papers without causing damage. The Gem paperclip's design was so successful that it quickly became the dominant form of paperclip, rendering many earlier designs obsolete.

The Gem paperclip's rise to prominence was facilitated by the advent of new manufacturing techniques that made it possible to produce the clips quickly and inexpensively. Advances in metalworking, particularly in the production of wire, allowed manufacturers to produce large quantities of paperclips with consistent quality and at a low cost. By the early 20th century, paperclips had become an essential item in offices and homes around the world, and their simple, functional design set the standard for paper fasteners for decades to come.

The paperclip's utility extended beyond its primary function of holding papers together. During World War II, the paperclip became a symbol of resistance and solidarity in Nazi-occupied Norway. Norwegians wore paperclips on their clothing as a subtle yet powerful symbol of unity and opposition to the occupation. The paperclip's symbolic role in this context highlights its versatility and cultural significance, transcending its everyday use as a mere office supply.

The post-war period saw further refinements in paperclip design and materials. The standard Gem paperclip, made from steel or other metals, continued to dominate the market, but new variations and improvements emerged as well. Some paperclips were coated with plastic to provide additional protection against rust and to add a touch of color, while others were made from different metals or alloys to offer enhanced durability or flexibility. The basic design of the paperclip, however, remained largely unchanged, a testament to the ingenuity and effectiveness of the original Gem design.

The paperclip's enduring popularity and widespread use can be attributed to its simplicity, versatility, and efficiency. Unlike other methods of fastening papers, such as staples or adhesives, paperclips do not damage the documents they hold and can be easily removed and reused. They are also inexpensive and readily available, making them an ideal solution for a wide range of organizational needs. The paperclip's design allows it to hold papers of varying thickness and size, and it can be used in a variety of contexts, from offices and schools to homes and workshops.

In addition to its practical applications, the paperclip has also found a place in art and culture. Artists and designers have used paperclips as a medium for creative expression, crafting intricate sculptures, jewelry, and other objects from the humble clips. The paperclip's simple yet elegant form has inspired a range of artistic interpretations, reflecting its unique combination of functionality and aesthetic appeal.

The paperclip has also been the subject of numerous patents and innovations over the years. While the basic design of the Gem paperclip remains the most popular, inventors and designers have continued to explore new ways to improve and adapt the paperclip for different uses. Some of these innovations have included variations in the shape and size of the clip, the use of different materials, and the incorporation of additional features such as magnets or built-in rulers. These variations highlight the ongoing relevance and adaptability of the paperclip in an ever-changing world.

The paperclip's role in modern society extends beyond its practical uses and cultural significance. It has also become a symbol of ingenuity and resourcefulness, representing the power of simple solutions to solve complex problems.

In recent years, the paperclip has also become a symbol of innovation and creativity in the digital age. The term "paperclip" has been used metaphorically to describe software tools and features that help users organize and manage digital documents and information. This modern use of the paperclip as a symbol of digital organization reflects its enduring relevance and adaptability in a rapidly changing world.

Chapter 4: The Story Behind the Zipper

The zipper, a commonplace yet crucial fastening device, is an invention that revolutionized the way we dress, carry, and secure objects. Its development spans over a century and includes numerous innovations, patent battles, and shifts in fashion and technology. The zipper's story is a fascinating journey of persistence, creativity, and transformative design that has left an indelible mark on modern life.

The history of the zipper begins in the 19th century with the advent of industrialization, which spurred the need for more efficient and convenient fastening methods for clothing and other items. Before the zipper, buttons, hooks, and laces were the primary means of fastening garments. While these methods were effective, they were often time-consuming and cumbersome, prompting inventors to seek alternatives.

The first significant step towards the invention of the zipper was taken in 1851 by Elias Howe, an American inventor best known for his contributions to the sewing machine. Howe patented a device he called the "Automatic, Continuous Clothing Closure," which featured a series of clasps joined by a cord running through eyelets. This early design, while innovative, was not practical and never went into production. Howe's focus remained on the sewing machine, and he did not pursue the development of his fastening device further.

It wasn't until the late 19th century that the zipper's development began to gain momentum. In 1891, Whitcomb L. Judson, another American inventor, patented a "Clasp Locker" designed to close shoes. Judson's device used a series of hooks and eyes and was intended to be a fast and efficient way to fasten boots and shoes. The Clasp Locker featured a sliding mechanism that brought the hooks and eyes together, much like a modern zipper. Despite its promise, Judson's invention was cumbersome and unreliable, prone to jamming and coming apart. However, Judson's efforts laid the foundation for future innovations.

In 1893, Judson's Clasp Locker made its debut at the Chicago World's Fair, where it garnered attention but failed to achieve commercial success. Undeterred, Judson continued to refine his design and in 1896 partnered with businessman Lewis Walker to form the Universal Fastener Company. Despite their efforts, the Clasp Locker remained a niche product, used primarily in boots and galoshes, and did not achieve widespread adoption.

The breakthrough that would transform the zipper into a practical and reliable device came in the early 20th century, thanks to the work of Gideon Sundback, a Swedish-American engineer. Sundback joined the Universal Fastener Company in 1906 and quickly set to work improving Judson's design. By 1913, Sundback had developed a new version of the zipper that featured a series of interlocking teeth made of metal, which were joined by a sliding mechanism. This new design was more robust and reliable than previous versions, solving many of the issues that had plagued earlier models.

Sundback's zipper, originally called the "Separable Fastener," was patented in 1917. The design consisted of two rows of interlocking teeth attached to fabric tapes and a slider that meshed the teeth together. The key innovation in Sundback's design was the use of metal teeth that could lock together securely, providing a smooth and dependable fastening mechanism. This new zipper was not only more functional but also easier to use, marking a significant advancement in fastening technology.

Despite its improved design, the zipper did not immediately gain widespread acceptance. Early applications of the zipper were limited to niche markets, such as military uniforms and specialty clothing, where the benefits of a secure and quick fastening mechanism were particularly valuable. It wasn't until the 1920s and 1930s that the zipper began to find broader applications in everyday clothing and accessories.

One of the first major breakthroughs for the zipper came in 1923 when the B. F. Goodrich Company, a prominent American tire and rubber manufacturer, decided to use zippers on its new line of rubber boots. Goodrich branded these boots "Zippers," a name that quickly caught on and eventually became synonymous with the fastener itself. The use of zippers in Goodrich's boots helped to popularize the device and demonstrated its practical advantages over traditional laces and buttons.

The zipper's popularity continued to grow in the 1930s, thanks in large part to its adoption by the fashion industry. Designers and manufacturers began to recognize the zipper's potential as a convenient and stylish alternative to buttons and hooks. The zipper's ability to provide a sleek, streamlined look was particularly appealing for garments such as skirts, dresses, and trousers. By the late 1930s, zippers were being used in a wide range of clothing, from everyday wear to high-fashion couture.

The zipper's versatility and reliability made it an ideal choice for a variety of applications beyond clothing. In the 1930s and 1940s, zippers began to be used in luggage, bags, tents, and other items where a secure and easy-to-use fastening mechanism was essential. The zipper's adaptability to different materials and its ability to withstand various environmental conditions further cemented its status as a vital component in numerous products.

World War II marked a significant period of growth for the zipper, as it was widely used in military uniforms and equipment. The war effort required efficient and durable fasteners for clothing, tents, and gear, and the zipper's reliability made it an ideal choice. The widespread use of zippers during the war helped to further increase their visibility and acceptance, paving the way for their post-war popularity.

The post-war period saw a dramatic expansion in the use of zippers across various industries. Advances in materials and manufacturing techniques allowed for the production of zippers in different sizes, colors, and styles, catering to a wide range of needs and preferences. The development of plastic zippers in the 1950s and 1960s provided an alternative to metal zippers, offering greater flexibility, corrosion resistance, and lower production costs. Plastic zippers quickly became popular in applications such as clothing, luggage, and sports equipment.

The zipper's influence extended beyond its practical applications, as it became a symbol of modernity and innovation. The sleek, functional design of the zipper was celebrated as a hallmark of mid-20th-century industrial design, and its presence in clothing and accessories reflected the era's emphasis on convenience and efficiency. The zipper's rise to prominence was emblematic of broader trends in fashion, technology, and consumer culture, highlighting the ways in which a simple invention can have a profound impact on daily life.

In the latter half of the 20th century, the zipper continued to evolve, with ongoing innovations in materials, design, and manufacturing. The introduction of coil zippers in the 1960s, which used a continuous coil of plastic or metal for the teeth, provided a new level of flexibility and ease of use. Coil zippers quickly became popular in applications requiring lightweight and flexible fasteners, such as outdoor gear and sportswear.

The zipper's role in the fashion industry also continued to expand, with designers experimenting with new ways to incorporate zippers into their creations. The zipper became a key element in the design of avant-garde and high-fashion garments, often used not just for its functional properties but also as a decorative and stylistic feature. The use of exposed zippers, asymmetrical designs, and unique fastening arrangements highlighted the zipper's potential as a design element, adding a modern and edgy aesthetic to clothing and accessories.

In addition to its impact on fashion and design, the zipper has played a significant role in various technological and industrial applications. Zippers are used in a wide range of products, from aerospace and automotive components to medical devices and consumer electronics. The development of specialized zippers, such as waterproof and fire-resistant zippers, has expanded the range of applications in which zippers can be used, highlighting their versatility and adaptability.

Chapter 5: The Invention of the Light Bulb

The invention of the light bulb stands as one of the most transformative achievements in human history, marking a monumental leap in technology that revolutionized how we live, work, and interact with our environment. The light bulb's journey from conceptual beginnings to its widespread adoption is a complex tale that encompasses numerous inventors, technological breakthroughs, and societal changes. Its development spanned decades, involving persistent experimentation, legal battles, and significant advances in materials and electrical engineering.

The story of the light bulb begins long before Thomas Edison, often credited with its invention. The quest to create a practical electric light started in the early 19th century, driven by the need for safer, more reliable lighting solutions compared to candles, oil lamps, and gas lamps, which were prone to causing fires and produced inefficient and often dim light.

One of the earliest pioneers in the development of electric lighting was Humphry Davy, an English scientist who, in 1800, discovered that passing an electric current through a piece of platinum produced light. This was achieved using an electric arc between two carbon rods, a principle that Davy demonstrated in 1809 with his invention of the electric arc lamp. While Davy's arc lamp was too bright and impractical for everyday use, it laid the groundwork for future innovations by proving that electricity could be used to generate light.

The next significant advance came in 1841 when British scientist Frederick de Moleyns received the first patent for an incandescent lamp. De Moleyns' design used a platinum filament enclosed in a vacuum to prevent it from burning out. Although this was a step forward, the lamp's high cost and limited durability prevented it from being commercially viable. Subsequent inventors continued to experiment with various materials and designs in an effort to create a more practical and reliable electric light.

In 1845, American inventor John W. Starr patented an incandescent lamp using carbon filaments, which are considered more durable and practical than previous designs. Unfortunately, Starr died shortly after obtaining his patent, and his work did not progress further. Another notable figure in the development of the light bulb was Warren de la Rue, a British chemist who, in 1841, created a lamp using a coiled platinum filament inside a vacuum. De la Rue's lamp was more efficient than previous designs, but the high cost of platinum made it impractical for widespread use.

The mid-19th century saw continued experimentation with various materials and designs, but it was not until the 1870s that significant progress was made towards a commercially viable light bulb. One of the key breakthroughs during this period was the development of improved vacuum technology, which allowed for the creation of more efficient and longer-lasting light bulbs. By removing air from the bulb, inventors were able to prevent the filament from oxidizing and burning out, a critical step in creating a durable light source.

In 1878, English physicist Sir Joseph Swan developed a working incandescent lamp using a carbonized paper filament inside a vacuum. Swan's lamp was demonstrated to the public in 1879, and he received a British patent for his invention. Swan's design was a significant improvement over earlier attempts, and he went on to install electric lighting in homes and public buildings, including the Savoy Theatre in London, which became the first public building in the world to be lit by electricity.

Around the same time, across the Atlantic, Thomas Edison was conducting his own experiments to develop a practical electric light. Edison, a prolific inventor and entrepreneur, was determined to create a commercially viable incandescent lamp that could replace gas lighting in homes and businesses. He focused on finding a filament material that was both durable and inexpensive, experimenting with hundreds of different substances, including bamboo, cotton, and even hair.

In 1879, after extensive testing, Edison and his team at Menlo Park finally succeeded in creating a light bulb that used a carbonized bamboo filament, which could last for up to 1,200 hours. Edison received a U.S. patent for his light bulb design in 1880, and his invention quickly gained widespread attention and acclaim. Unlike earlier designs, Edison's light bulb was practical, reliable, and affordable, making it accessible to the general public.

Edison's success was not without controversy, as it led to a series of legal battles over patent rights and the true origins of the light bulb. Edison and Swan both claimed to have invented the incandescent lamp, leading to a patent dispute that was eventually resolved in 1883 when the two inventors formed a joint venture, the Edison & Swan United Electric Light Company. This partnership helped to consolidate their contributions and further promote the widespread adoption of electric lighting.

The invention of the light bulb had profound implications for society, transforming the way people lived and worked. Electric lighting extended the length of the workday, allowing factories to operate around the clock and enabling businesses to stay open longer. It also made homes safer and more comfortable, reducing the risk of fire and providing a steady, reliable source of light. The advent of electric street lighting improved public safety and facilitated urbanization by making cities more livable after dark.

The rapid adoption of electric lighting also spurred the development of electrical infrastructure, including power plants, distribution networks, and electrical appliances. Edison's establishment of the Pearl Street Station in New York City in 1882 marked the beginning of the modern electric utility industry, providing power to homes and businesses and laying the foundation for the electrification of the world.

The early 20th century saw continued advancements in light bulb technology, driven by the demand for more efficient and longer-lasting lighting solutions. In 1906, the General Electric Company, founded by Edison, introduced the first tungsten filament light bulb. Tungsten, with its high melting point and excellent conductivity, proved to be an ideal material for filaments, allowing bulbs to operate at higher temperatures and produce brighter light. Tungsten filament bulbs quickly became the standard in the industry, replacing earlier carbon filament designs.

The development of the incandescent light bulb also paved the way for other forms of electric lighting, including fluorescent and LED technologies. Fluorescent lamps, first demonstrated in the early 20th century, offered greater energy efficiency and longer lifespans than incandescent bulbs, making them popular for commercial and industrial applications. The introduction of compact fluorescent lamps (CFLs) in the 1980s brought these benefits to the consumer market, further reducing energy consumption and promoting environmental sustainability.

The invention of the light-emitting diode (LED) in the 1960s marked another significant milestone in the evolution of electric lighting. LEDs, which produce light through the movement of electrons in a semiconductor material, offer even greater efficiency and durability than fluorescent lamps. The widespread adoption of LED technology in the early 21st century has revolutionized lighting once again, providing a highly energy-efficient and environmentally friendly alternative to traditional light sources.

The impact of the light bulb extends beyond its technological and economic significance. It has also played a crucial role in shaping modern culture and society. The ability to control and extend light has transformed how we perceive and interact with the world, influencing everything from art and entertainment to education and healthcare. The light bulb's invention has enabled the development of new technologies and industries, from photography and film to medical imaging and telecommunications.

25

Chapter 6: The Legacy of the Ballpoint Pen

The ballpoint pen, a ubiquitous tool in the modern world, holds a legacy that is deeply intertwined with the evolution of communication, technology, and culture. Its invention and subsequent rise to prominence reflect a journey of innovation, perseverance, and adaptation that has left an indelible mark on society.

The origins of the ballpoint pen can be traced back to the early 20th century, although the quest for a reliable and convenient writing instrument began much earlier. Before the ballpoint pen, quill pens, dip pens, and fountain pens were the primary tools for writing. These instruments required frequent dipping into ink, were prone to leaking, and often produced inconsistent writing. The need for a more practical and efficient writing tool was evident, especially as the pace of business and communication accelerated in the modern world.

The first significant steps towards the invention of the ballpoint pen were taken by John J. Loud, an American inventor, in 1888. Loud, who was a leather tanner, sought to create a pen that could write on rough surfaces such as leather. He devised a pen with a rotating ball bearing in its tip that was held in place by a socket, which would pick up ink from an internal reservoir and transfer it to the writing surface. Loud's invention, while innovative, was not practical for everyday writing on paper due to issues with ink flow and the tendency of the pen to leak. Consequently, his invention did not gain commercial success, and the idea of the ballpoint pen languished for several decades.

The breakthrough that would transform the ballpoint pen into a practical writing instrument came in the 1930s, thanks to the efforts of a Hungarian journalist named László Bíró. Bíró, frustrated by the smudging and frequent refilling required by fountain pens, sought a better solution. He noticed that newspaper ink dried quickly and did not smudge, which inspired him to develop a pen that used a similar type of ink. Working with his brother György, a chemist, László Bíró developed a new ink formula that was thicker and more viscous than traditional fountain pen ink, allowing it to dry quickly and resist smudging.

In 1938, Bíró patented his design for a ballpoint pen that used a small rotating ball in the tip to pick up ink from an internal reservoir and transfer it to the paper. The ball, made of steel, was held in place by a socket that allowed it to rotate freely, drawing ink from the reservoir and spreading it evenly on the writing surface. Bíró's design solved many of the problems that had plagued earlier attempts at ballpoint pens, such as leakage and inconsistent ink flow, and provided a smooth and reliable writing experience.

Bíró's invention quickly gained attention, and he began producing ballpoint pens in Argentina, where he had emigrated during World War II. The pens, marketed under the brand name "Birome," became popular for their convenience and reliability, particularly among military personnel who needed a durable and efficient writing tool. The success of Bíró's ballpoint pen in Argentina laid the foundation for its eventual global adoption and commercialization.

The commercial potential of the ballpoint pen was recognized by several entrepreneurs and companies, leading to a flurry of patents, legal battles, and innovations in the 1940s and 1950s. One of the key figures in the commercialization of the ballpoint pen was Milton Reynolds, an American businessman who, in 1945, saw a Birome pen during a trip to Argentina. Recognizing its potential, Reynolds bought several pens and brought them back to the United States, where he reverse-engineered the design and began producing his own version under the brand name "Reynolds Rocket."

Reynolds' ballpoint pen, introduced in 1945, was an immediate sensation, selling out quickly despite its high price of $12.50

(equivalent to over $150 today). The success of the Reynolds Rocket spurred other companies to enter the market, leading to fierce competition and rapid advancements in ballpoint pen technology. One of the major players in this emerging industry was the Eberhard Faber Company, which developed its own version of the ballpoint pen and marketed it as a reliable and affordable alternative to the Reynolds Rocket.

The race to dominate the ballpoint pen market led to significant improvements in design, materials, and manufacturing processes. By the late 1940s, several companies, including Parker and Sheaffer, had introduced their own ballpoint pens, each claiming superior performance and reliability. These early ballpoint pens were still relatively expensive and prone to issues such as ink leakage and inconsistent writing, but they represented a significant step forward in the development of a practical and convenient writing instrument.

The pivotal moment in the history of the ballpoint pen came in the early 1950s with the entry of Marcel Bich, a French industrialist and founder of Société Bic. Bich recognized the need for a high-quality, mass-produced ballpoint pen that was affordable and reliable. In 1950, he acquired the patent rights to Bíró's ballpoint pen design and set out to improve the manufacturing process. Bich's innovations in materials and production techniques allowed him to produce ballpoint pens at a fraction of the cost of his competitors, without sacrificing quality.

In 1953, Bich introduced the Bic Cristal, a disposable ballpoint pen that quickly became a global bestseller. The Bic Cristal featured a clear plastic barrel, allowing users to see the ink level, and a hexagonal shape that provided a comfortable grip. It's simple, reliable design and low cost made it accessible to a wide audience, transforming the ballpoint pen from a luxury item into an everyday essential. The success of the Bic Cristal revolutionized the writing instrument industry, leading to the widespread adoption of ballpoint pens around the world.

The impact of the ballpoint pen on society and culture cannot be overstated. Its convenience, reliability, and affordability made it an indispensable tool for students, professionals, and everyday users, facilitating communication, education, and creativity. The ballpoint pen's durability and ease of use also made it ideal for use in challenging environments, from military operations to space missions, where traditional pens would be impractical or unreliable.

The ballpoint pen's influence extends beyond its practical applications, shaping the way we think about writing and communication. Its introduction coincided with significant changes in education and literacy, contributing to the democratization of knowledge and the spread of information. The affordability and accessibility of ballpoint pens made writing tools available to a broader population, supporting the expansion of education and literacy in both developed and developing countries.

The ballpoint pen also played a significant role in the development of new forms of artistic expression. Its versatility and ease of use made it a popular medium for artists and illustrators, who used it to create detailed drawings and intricate designs. The ballpoint pen's unique characteristics, such as its ability to produce fine lines and varying shades of ink, inspired new techniques and styles, contributing to the evolution of contemporary art.

The environmental impact of the ballpoint pen has also been a topic of discussion and concern. The widespread use of disposable ballpoint pens has contributed to the accumulation of plastic waste, prompting calls for more sustainable alternatives. In response, manufacturers have developed reusable and refillable ballpoint pens, as well as pens made from recycled materials, to reduce their environmental footprint. The shift towards more sustainable practices reflects a growing awareness of the need to balance convenience with environmental responsibility.

The legacy of the ballpoint pen is also evident in its influence on other writing instruments and technologies. The principles behind the ballpoint pen's design have inspired the development of new types of pens, such as gel pens and rollerball pens, which offer different writing experiences and cater to diverse preferences. The ballpoint pen's emphasis on practicality and reliability has also influenced the design of electronic writing devices, such as styluses for tablets and smartphones, which aim to combine the convenience of digital technology with the tactile experience of traditional writing.

The continued relevance of the ballpoint pen in the digital age highlights its enduring appeal and versatility. Despite the proliferation of digital communication tools, the ballpoint pen remains a popular and reliable choice for writing and note-taking, valued for its simplicity, portability, and ease of use. Its ability to provide a tangible, personal connection to the act of writing has ensured its place as a timeless and indispensable tool in our daily lives.

Chapter 7: The History of the Eraser

The history of the eraser, a small yet indispensable tool in the world of writing and drawing, is a fascinating tale of innovation, scientific discovery, and practical application that spans centuries and continents. The eraser's journey from its rudimentary beginnings to its modern form reflects broader developments in materials science, industrialization, and education, revealing how a simple object can have a profound impact on human creativity and communication.

The concept of erasing mistakes predates the invention of the eraser by millennia. Ancient civilizations, such as the Egyptians and Greeks, sought various methods to correct writing errors. In these early societies, writing was typically done on papyrus or parchment using reeds or quills dipped in ink. When errors were made, scribes would use abrasive materials, such as sand, stones, or even pumice, to scrape away the ink and prepare the surface for rewriting. This laborious process required precision and care, as excessive abrasion could damage the writing surface, making it difficult to correct mistakes without leaving noticeable marks.

In ancient Rome, scribes employed a different approach to correction. Roman writing was often done on wax tablets using a stylus. When errors occurred, the scribe would use the flat end of the stylus to smooth the wax, effectively erasing the mistake and allowing for the surface to be reused. This method was relatively efficient and allowed for multiple corrections, but it was limited to wax-based writing surfaces and was not suitable for permanent documents.

The development of paper in China during the early centuries CE introduced new challenges for erasure. Traditional methods of scraping or smoothing were ineffective on paper, which required a more delicate touch. To address this, early Chinese scholars and calligraphers used bits of wet bread to gently blot out errors. This method, while somewhat effective, was far from perfect, as it often left behind smudges and residual marks. The use of bread for erasing continued in various forms across different cultures, highlighting the universal need for an effective way to correct mistakes in written work.

The quest for a more efficient eraser took a significant step forward in the 18th century with the advent of rubber, a material derived from the latex sap of rubber trees. Rubber was first introduced to Europe in the mid-1700s by European explorers returning from South America, where indigenous peoples had long used it for various purposes, including waterproofing and making balls. The French scientist Charles Marie de La Condamine, who led an expedition to the Amazon, was one of the first Europeans to study and document the properties of rubber, noting its potential applications in various fields.

In 1770, the British scientist and inventor Joseph Priestley made a groundbreaking discovery that would change the course of eraser history. Priestley found that a piece of natural rubber could effectively remove pencil marks from paper, an observation that led him to coin the term "rubber" for the material. Prior to this, pencil erasure was typically done using bread or other abrasive substances, which were far less effective and more damaging to the paper. Priestley's discovery highlighted the unique properties of rubber, including its elasticity and ability to grip and lift graphite particles without causing harm to the underlying surface.

Priestley's discovery quickly gained attention, and rubber erasers began to replace older methods of correction. Early rubber erasers were crude and had several drawbacks, including a tendency to crumble and an unpleasant odor due to the presence of impurities in the natural rubber. Despite these issues, the superiority of rubber over previous erasing materials was clear, and inventors and manufacturers began experimenting with ways to improve its properties and make it more suitable for widespread use.

One of the key figures in the development of the modern eraser was Edward Nairne, a British engineer and inventor who is often credited with creating the first commercial rubber eraser. In 1770, Nairne began selling rubber erasers in his London shop, marketing them as a superior alternative to bread for removing pencil marks. Nairne's erasers were initially quite expensive, costing around three shillings per cube, a significant amount at the time. Despite the cost, the demand for these new erasers grew, driven by their effectiveness and the increasing popularity of pencil writing.

The next major advancement in eraser technology came with the discovery of vulcanization, a process that revolutionized the rubber industry. In 1839, Charles Goodyear, an American inventor, accidentally discovered that heating natural rubber with sulfur transformed it into a more durable and elastic material. This process, known as vulcanization, significantly improved the properties of rubber, making it more resilient, stable, and less prone to decomposition. Vulcanized rubber was ideal for erasers, as it provided a consistent and effective means of removing pencil marks without crumbling or smearing.

The widespread adoption of vulcanized rubber in the mid-19th century led to the mass production of rubber erasers, making them more affordable and accessible to the general public. This period also saw the introduction of various innovations and improvements in eraser design, including the development of different shapes, sizes, and formulations to suit a range of needs and preferences. The iconic pink eraser, for example, was first introduced by the Eberhard Faber Company in the late 19th century and quickly became a staple in classrooms and offices around the world.

The integration of erasers into the tops of pencils marked another significant milestone in the history of the eraser. The first patent for a pencil with an attached eraser was granted to Hymen Lipman, an American inventor, in 1858. Lipman's design featured a rubber eraser inserted into the end of a wooden pencil, providing a convenient and efficient way to correct mistakes without the need for a separate tool.

This innovation was particularly popular in educational settings, where it simplified the process of writing and erasing for students.

Despite its success, Lipman's patent faced legal challenges, leading to a landmark court case that ultimately invalidated the patent on the grounds that it was merely a combination of two existing products. Nevertheless, the concept of the pencil with an attached eraser proved to be a lasting and influential innovation, and it continued to be produced and refined by various manufacturers. The popularity of this design highlights the importance of convenience and practicality in the evolution of writing tools and erasers.

The 20th century saw further advancements in eraser technology, driven by developments in materials science and manufacturing techniques. Synthetic rubbers, such as styrene-butadiene and polyurethane, were developed as alternatives to natural rubber, offering improved performance and consistency. These synthetic materials allowed for the production of erasers with specific properties, such as increased abrasion resistance and reduced smudging, tailored to different applications and user preferences.

The introduction of vinyl and plastic erasers in the mid-20th century marked another significant development in the history of the eraser. Vinyl erasers, made from polyvinyl chloride (PVC), offered superior durability and precision compared to traditional rubber erasers. They were particularly popular among artists and draftsmen, who valued their ability to make clean, precise corrections without damaging the paper. Plastic erasers, made from various synthetic polymers, also gained popularity for their effectiveness in removing graphite and ink without smearing or tearing the paper.

The evolution of eraser design and technology continued into the late 20th and early 21st centuries, with the introduction of specialized erasers for different types of writing and drawing. Kneaded erasers, made from a pliable material that can be shaped and molded, became popular among artists for their versatility and ability to lift graphite and charcoal without leaving residue. Electric erasers, featuring a motorized mechanism that rapidly rotates an eraser tip, provided a convenient solution for making precise corrections in technical drawing and drafting.

The legacy of the eraser extends beyond its practical applications, reflecting broader trends in education, art, and communication. The widespread availability of affordable and effective erasers has played a crucial role in supporting literacy and learning, making it easier for students to practice writing and correct mistakes. The eraser's significance in education is underscored by its presence in classrooms around the world, where it remains an essential tool for students of all ages.

In the realm of art and design, the eraser has become a valuable tool for creating and refining works of art. Artists use erasers not only to correct mistakes but also to achieve specific effects and textures, highlighting the eraser's versatility and creative potential. The eraser's role in art reflects the broader trend of repurposing everyday objects for artistic expression, demonstrating how a simple tool can be used to create complex and nuanced works of art.

The environmental impact of erasers has also become a topic of discussion in recent years, as concerns about plastic waste and sustainability have grown. Many traditional erasers are made from synthetic materials that do not biodegrade, contributing to the accumulation of plastic waste in landfills and oceans. In response, manufacturers have begun developing more sustainable alternatives, such as erasers made from biodegradable materials and recycled rubber. These efforts reflect a growing awareness of the need to balance the convenience and functionality of erasers with environmental responsibility.

The history of the eraser is a testament to the power of innovation and the importance of simple, practical solutions in everyday life. From its early beginnings as a piece of wet bread to its modern incarnation as a sophisticated tool made from advanced materials, the eraser has undergone a remarkable transformation. Its journey reflects broader trends in technological progress, consumer culture, and environmental awareness, highlighting the enduring value of innovation in shaping the tools we use and the world we live in.

The eraser's legacy is also a reminder of the importance of adaptability and resilience in the face of changing needs and challenges. The evolution of the eraser from a rudimentary correction tool to a highly specialized and versatile instrument demonstrates how human ingenuity can continually improve and refine even the simplest of objects. The eraser's story is a celebration of creativity and the pursuit of excellence, inspiring future generations to continue exploring new ways to enhance and enrich our lives.

Chapter 8: The Transformation of the Umbrella

The umbrella, a ubiquitous tool in modern life, has undergone significant transformations over millennia, reflecting changes in technology, culture, and society. The origins of the umbrella trace back to ancient civilizations, where it served not only as protection against the elements but also as a symbol of status and power. In ancient Egypt, around 1200 BC, umbrellas were primarily used to provide shade from the sun. These early versions, often depicted in art and hieroglyphs, were crafted from palm leaves or feathers and were reserved for royalty and high-ranking officials. The concept of the umbrella spread from Egypt to Assyria, China, and Greece, each culture adapting the design to their needs and climate.

In China, around the same period, the umbrella began to evolve into a more practical tool. The Chinese are credited with inventing the first waterproof umbrellas by applying wax and lacquer to paper umbrellas, making them effective against rain. This innovation was significant in a region with varied weather conditions. The use of umbrellas in China also had cultural and ceremonial importance, often symbolizing rank and used in various rituals and ceremonies. The spread of umbrellas to Japan and Korea further influenced their design and use, integrating local materials and craftsmanship techniques.

By the time the umbrella reached Greece and Rome, its function had expanded. In these Mediterranean climates, umbrellas continued to serve as sunshades but also began to be used in processions and public events. Greek women of the upper class often used parasols; a variation of the umbrella designed specifically to block the sun. These parasols were ornate, decorated with intricate designs and fabrics, highlighting their dual role as practical and fashion accessories. The

Romans, known for their engineering prowess, further refined the umbrella's design, making it collapsible and portable.

The Middle Ages saw a decline in the use of umbrellas in Europe, possibly due to the region's cooler climate and the fall of the Roman Empire, which led to a loss of many technological advancements. However, the Renaissance period brought a revival of the umbrella, particularly in Italy and France. This era's renewed interest in art, culture, and science spurred innovations in many areas, including personal accessories like the umbrella. Italian craftsmen began producing beautifully decorated umbrellas, often using silk and precious metals. These umbrellas were seen as luxury items and became popular among the European aristocracy.

The 17th century marked a significant turning point in the umbrella's history. In England, the use of umbrellas began to spread among the general population, largely due to the influence of the writer and philanthropist Jonas Hanway. Hanway was an advocate for the umbrella, using it regularly and promoting its practicality in London's often rainy weather. Despite initial ridicule, Hanway's persistence paid off, and by the late 18th century, umbrellas became a common sight in English cities. These early English umbrellas were quite large and heavy, often made with whalebone or cane ribs and covered with oiled silk to repel water.

The Industrial Revolution in the 19th century brought significant advancements to umbrella manufacturing. The development of new materials and production techniques made umbrellas more affordable and durable. Steel ribs replaced whalebone, making umbrellas lighter and more flexible. The introduction of mass production allowed for greater availability, and umbrellas became accessible to a wider range of people. This period also saw the development of the telescoping umbrella, which could be collapsed and easily carried, further enhancing its practicality.

In the late 19th and early 20th centuries, the design and function of umbrellas continued to evolve. The invention of the modern folding umbrella by Hans Haupt in 1928 revolutionized the market. Haupt's design, which used a combination of steel and aluminum ribs, was lightweight, compact, and easy to use. This innovation made umbrellas even more convenient and portable, solidifying their place as a staple in everyday life. Umbrellas also became a popular advertising medium, with companies printing their logos and slogans on the canopy, turning them into mobile billboards.

Throughout the 20th century, technological advancements and changing fashion trends continued to influence the umbrella's design. The introduction of synthetic materials such as nylon and polyester made umbrellas more water-resistant and durable. Ergonomic handles, automatic opening mechanisms, and wind-resistant designs further improved their functionality. Umbrellas also became a fashion statement, with designers creating a wide range of styles, colors, and patterns to suit different tastes and occasions.

Today, the umbrella remains an essential accessory worldwide, used by people of all ages and backgrounds. Its design has been refined to meet various needs, from compact travel umbrellas to large golf umbrellas. The development of high-tech materials and smart features, such as UV protection and built-in lights, continues to enhance its practicality and appeal. Despite these advancements, the basic concept of the umbrella has remained remarkably consistent, testament to its enduring utility and significance.

The transformation of the umbrella over thousands of years highlights the interplay between innovation, culture, and everyday life. From its origins as a symbol of status in ancient civilizations to its current status as a practical and stylish accessory, the umbrella's evolution reflects broader trends in technology, society, and human ingenuity. Whether shielding us from the sun or rain, the umbrella continues to be a testament to our ability to adapt and innovate, making it an indispensable part of our daily lives.

Chapter 9: The Innovation of the Paper Bag

The innovation of the paper bag represents a fascinating journey through technological advancements, societal shifts, and environmental considerations over more than a century. The paper bag, now a staple in retail and grocery stores, began its life in the mid-19th century as an alternative to cumbersome and often unreliable cloth or burlap sacks. This period marked the beginning of an industrial era where convenience and efficiency in packaging became increasingly important.

The first recorded patent for a paper bag machine was granted to Francis Wolle, a schoolteacher from Pennsylvania, in 1852. Wolle's invention was rudimentary by today's standards, but it laid the groundwork for future developments. His machine could produce simple, flat-bottomed paper bags at a rate much faster than hand production. This innovation not only increased production capacity but also reduced costs, making paper bags accessible to a broader market. Wolle later co-founded the Union Paper Bag Machine Company, which played a significant role in popularizing paper bags in the United States.

The next significant leap in paper bag innovation came from Margaret Knight in 1868. Knight, an employee at the Columbia Paper Bag Company, invented a machine that could produce square-bottomed bags, which were far more practical for carrying items as they could stand upright and hold more content. Her design included a sophisticated set of components that cut, folded, and glued the paper, creating a durable and stable bag. Knight's invention was so transformative that it earned her a patent in 1871, marking her as one of the first women to receive a patent for a major industrial invention.

In the early 20th century, the paper bag continued to evolve with the invention of the self-opening square (SOS) bag by Charles Stilwell in 1883. Stilwell's design included pleated sides, which allowed the bags to be easily folded and stacked, saving space and making them more convenient for both retailers and consumers. These bags could also be produced in various sizes, further enhancing their versatility. Stilwell's invention underscored the ongoing quest for practicality and efficiency in packaging.

The 20th century also saw advancements in the materials and processes used in paper bag production. The development of kraft paper, a strong, durable paper made from wood pulp, significantly improved the quality and strength of paper bags. Kraft paper, developed by Carl F. Dahl in the 1870s, undergoes a chemical process that removes lignin from the wood fibers, resulting in a more robust and tear-resistant product. This advancement allowed paper bags to carry heavier items, further solidifying their place in the market.

As the century progressed, the use of paper bags expanded beyond retail and groceries to a variety of other industries, including food service and shipping. The introduction of reinforced handles, multi-ply construction, and moisture-resistant coatings enabled paper bags to meet the demands of different applications. For instance, paper bags with wax coatings became popular for carrying hot and greasy foods, while multi-layered bags were used for products like flour and cement.

The environmental movement of the late 20th century brought new attention to the use of paper bags. As concerns about plastic pollution grew, paper bags were often touted as a more eco-friendly alternative to plastic bags. The renewable nature of paper, along with its biodegradability and recyclability, made it an attractive option for environmentally conscious consumers and businesses. However, the production of paper bags also faced scrutiny due to deforestation and the energy-intensive processes involved in manufacturing. This led to increased efforts to source sustainable materials and improve the efficiency of production methods.

In response to these environmental challenges, the paper bag industry has made significant strides in recent years. Innovations in recycling technology have allowed for a greater percentage of post-consumer recycled content in paper bags, reducing the demand for virgin pulp. Additionally, sustainable forestry practices have been implemented to ensure that the wood used in paper bag production comes from responsibly managed forests. Certifications such as the Forest Stewardship Council (FSC) label help consumers identify products that meet these rigorous standards.

The digital age has also influenced the paper bag industry, with advances in design and printing technology enabling high-quality, customizable bags for branding and marketing purposes. Companies can now produce paper bags with intricate designs, vibrant colors, and even interactive elements like QR codes. This has turned paper bags into not just a practical item but also a powerful tool for brand promotion and customer engagement.

Moreover, the resurgence of the "reduce, reuse, recycle" ethos has led to creative and innovative uses for paper bags beyond their primary function. Craft enthusiasts and educators have embraced paper bags for various projects, from gift wrapping and decorations to educational tools and storage solutions. This versatility highlights the enduring value of the paper bag in both practical and imaginative contexts.

The rise of e-commerce has also impacted the paper bag industry. With the increase in online shopping, there has been a growing demand for sustainable packaging solutions for shipping and delivery. Paper bags, with their strength and eco-friendly attributes, are increasingly being used as protective packaging for a wide range of products, from clothing to electronics. The industry has responded by developing more durable and customizable paper bags to meet the specific needs of online retailers and their customers.

Chapter 10: The Journey of the Rubber Band

The journey of the rubber band is a testament to human ingenuity and the ability to find novel solutions to everyday problems. This small but incredibly useful object has a rich history, rooted in ancient civilizations and spanning through significant technological and scientific advancements. From its primitive beginnings to its modern-day applications, the rubber band has evolved in fascinating ways.

The story of the rubber band begins with the discovery of natural rubber, which is derived from the latex sap of certain trees, most notably the Hevea brasiliensis, or rubber tree. Indigenous peoples of Mesoamerica, including the Olmec, Maya, and Aztec civilizations, were the first to discover the properties of natural rubber. They used the latex to create various items, including waterproof footwear, containers, and balls for their ceremonial games. The process involved collecting the sap and letting it coagulate, then molding it into desired shapes.

The introduction of natural rubber to Europe in the 16th century, following the exploration of the New World, marked the beginning of its global journey. However, it wasn't until the 19th century that significant advancements in rubber processing occurred. The problem with natural rubber was its susceptibility to temperature changes, becoming sticky in heat and brittle in cold. This limitation hindered its practical applications.

The turning point came with the discovery of vulcanization by Charles Goodyear in 1839. Vulcanization is a chemical process that involves heating rubber with sulfur, which creates cross-links between polymer chains, enhancing the material's elasticity, strength, and durability. This breakthrough transformed rubber into a versatile material suitable for a wide range of uses, from industrial applications to everyday products.

In the mid-19th century, the first rubber bands were invented by Stephen Perry, an English businessman and inventor. Perry's company, Messrs Perry and Co, was already producing rubber items, and he saw the potential for creating a product that could hold items together. In 1845, Perry patented the rubber band, which was made by slicing tubes of vulcanized rubber into rings. This simple yet ingenious idea quickly gained popularity, as rubber bands were found to be useful for bundling papers, securing packages, and countless other tasks.

As rubber band production increased, so did the demand for rubber. This led to the establishment of rubber plantations in tropical regions, particularly in Southeast Asia. The British Empire played a significant role in this expansion, with British planters introducing rubber cultivation to Malaysia, which eventually became one of the world's largest producers of natural rubber. The development of these plantations was driven by the burgeoning demand for rubber in various industries, including automotive, manufacturing, and consumer goods.

The early 20th century saw further innovations in rubber band manufacturing. The introduction of synthetic rubber during World War II was a pivotal moment. Natural rubber supplies were severely disrupted during the war, prompting extensive research into synthetic alternatives. Chemists developed synthetic rubber from petroleum-based materials, which not only provided a reliable substitute during wartime shortages but also offered additional benefits such as improved resistance to chemicals and extreme temperatures. This development expanded the range of applications for rubber bands and ensured a steady supply.

In the post-war era, the rubber band continued to evolve, with improvements in both materials and production techniques. The invention of continuous manufacturing processes allowed for the mass production of rubber bands, making them more affordable and widely available. These processes involved extruding rubber into long tubes, which were then cut into bands of various sizes. The ability to produce rubber bands in large quantities revolutionized their use, making them an indispensable tool in offices, homes, and industries around the world.

The versatility of rubber bands has led to their adoption in a wide array of applications beyond their original purpose. In agriculture, rubber bands are used to bundle and secure produce, while in the medical field, they are employed in various devices and procedures. Orthodontists, for example, use small rubber bands to apply pressure and guide the movement of teeth during treatment. Rubber bands are also essential components in the packaging and logistics industries, helping to secure items during transport and storage.

The environmental impact of rubber band production has become an area of focus in recent years. The reliance on both natural and synthetic rubber raises concerns about sustainability and environmental footprint. Natural rubber production involves deforestation and habitat loss in tropical regions, while synthetic rubber production is dependent on fossil fuels and generates chemical waste. In response to these challenges, researchers and manufacturers are exploring eco-friendly alternatives and practices.

One approach is the development of biodegradable rubber bands made from natural latex and other renewable materials. These bands are designed to break down more easily in the environment, reducing the long-term impact of discarded rubber products. Additionally, efforts are being made to improve the sustainability of rubber plantations through responsible land management, reforestation, and the use of sustainable agricultural practices.

Another area of innovation is the recycling of rubber bands. While traditional recycling methods for rubber are complex and energy-intensive, new techniques are being developed to repurpose used rubber bands into new products. This not only helps to reduce waste but also provides an alternative source of material for rubber band production. Consumers and businesses are also encouraged to reuse rubber bands whenever possible, extending their lifespan and minimizing waste.

The rubber band's journey from ancient Mesoamerican civilizations to modern-day ubiquity is a remarkable tale of innovation and adaptation. Its evolution has been driven by advances in science and technology, shifts in global trade and industry, and growing awareness of environmental sustainability. Despite its simplicity, the rubber band continues to be a vital tool with diverse applications, demonstrating the enduring value of this humble invention.

Chapter 11: The Genesis of the Coffee Mug

The genesis of the coffee mug is a captivating journey that spans across centuries, cultures, and technological advancements. This seemingly simple object, which today is an essential part of daily life for millions of people around the world, has a rich and varied history that reflects broader trends in human civilization, from the dawn of pottery to the modern era of mass production and design innovation.

The earliest precursors to the coffee mug can be traced back to ancient civilizations that first developed pottery techniques. Around 20,000 years ago, during the late Paleolithic era, the first ceramic vessels appeared in China. These early pieces were hand-built and fired at low temperatures, making them porous and fragile. Despite these limitations, they represented a significant technological advancement, enabling people to store and transport liquids more effectively than before.

By the time of the Neolithic Revolution, around 10,000 BCE, pottery had become more widespread and sophisticated. In the Near East, communities began settling in one place and developing agriculture, which led to the creation of permanent settlements and the need for durable, functional vessels. The invention of the potter's wheel around 3,500 BCE in Mesopotamia revolutionized pottery, allowing for more uniform and finely crafted pieces. These advancements laid the groundwork for the development of various types of cups and mugs.

In ancient Egypt and Mesopotamia, drinking vessels were crafted from clay, metal, and even stone. These early cups were often elaborately decorated and used in both daily life and religious ceremonies. The Greeks and Romans further refined the art of pottery, creating beautifully decorated cups and bowls made from clay and glass.

The Romans, in particular, were known for their glassware, which was prized for its beauty and utility.

The use of mugs specifically for coffee can be traced to the introduction of coffee to the Arab world in the 15th century. Coffee is believed to have originated in Ethiopia, where it was discovered by the Oromo people. By the 15th century, coffee had spread to Yemen, where Sufi monks used it to stay awake during their nocturnal devotions. The beverage quickly gained popularity, and coffeehouses, known as qahveh khaneh, began to appear in cities throughout the Islamic world. These establishments served as social hubs where people could gather to drink coffee, discuss politics, and enjoy music and poetry.

The mugs used in these early coffeehouses were typically made from ceramics and were often simple in design. The primary focus was on functionality, as the vessels needed to withstand the heat of the coffee and be durable enough for frequent use. However, as coffee culture spread, so did the variety and sophistication of the mugs used to serve it.

Coffee reached Europe in the 17th century, where it quickly became a popular beverage. The first European coffeehouse opened in Venice in 1645, and soon, coffeehouses were established in major cities across the continent. In England, the first coffeehouse opened in Oxford in 1650, followed by London in 1652. These establishments became centers of intellectual exchange, attracting scholars, writers, and politicians.

The demand for coffee and the vessels to serve it in led to significant developments in European pottery and ceramics. One of the most notable innovations was the creation of porcelain. Originating in China during the Tang Dynasty (618–907 CE), porcelain was highly prized for its strength, translucence, and beauty. European potters long sought to replicate Chinese porcelain, and in the early 18th century, they succeeded. Johann Friedrich Böttger, working in the court of Augustus the Strong in Saxony, discovered the formula for hard-paste porcelain. This breakthrough led to the establishment of the Meissen porcelain factory in 1710, which produced some of the finest coffee mugs and cups of the era.

The 18th and 19th centuries saw the proliferation of porcelain and ceramic coffee mugs across Europe and America. Factories such as Meissen, Wedgwood in England, and Limoges in France produced a wide range of coffee mugs, from the plain and utilitarian to the highly decorative and luxurious. These mugs often featured intricate designs, including floral patterns, pastoral scenes, and classical motifs, reflecting the artistic tastes of the time.

The Industrial Revolution brought significant changes to the production of coffee mugs. Advances in manufacturing technology allowed for the mass production of ceramics, making coffee mugs more affordable and accessible to a broader population. The development of transfer printing in the mid-18th century revolutionized the decoration of ceramics, allowing for detailed designs to be applied quickly and consistently. This period also saw the introduction of new materials, such as bone china, which combined the strength of porcelain with a more delicate appearance.

In the 20th century, the coffee mug underwent further transformation, influenced by changes in design, culture, and technology. The rise of the modernist movement in the early 20th century brought a focus on simplicity, functionality, and clean lines. Designers like the Bauhaus school in Germany emphasized the form and utility of everyday objects, including coffee mugs. This period also saw the introduction of new materials, such as heat-resistant glass and plastics, which expanded the possibilities for coffee mug design.

The mid-20th century was marked by the rise of branded and promotional coffee mugs. As coffee consumption continued to grow, businesses recognized the potential of coffee mugs as marketing tools. Companies began producing mugs with their logos and slogans, turning them into promotional items and souvenirs. This trend continues to this day, with branded coffee mugs being a common sight in homes and offices around the world.

The late 20th and early 21st centuries have seen a resurgence of interest in artisanal and handmade coffee mugs. As part of a broader movement towards sustainability and authenticity, many people have sought out unique, handcrafted mugs made by local artisans. This trend has been supported by the rise of online marketplaces, which have made it easier for independent potters to reach a global audience.

The modern coffee mug comes in an astonishing variety of shapes, sizes, and materials. While ceramic remains a popular choice due to its durability and heat retention properties, mugs are also made from glass, stainless steel, and even bamboo. Innovations such as double-walled mugs provide additional insulation, keeping coffee hot for longer periods. The design of coffee mugs continues to evolve, influenced by trends in art, fashion, and technology.

One notable recent development is the integration of smart technology into coffee mugs. Some modern mugs come equipped with features such as temperature control, allowing users to set and maintain their preferred coffee temperature. Others include built-in stirring mechanisms, spill-proof lids, and even charging capabilities for electronic devices. These innovations reflect the ongoing quest to enhance the coffee-drinking experience and meet the needs of today's tech-savvy consumers.

The environmental impact of coffee mug production has also become a significant consideration in recent years. As awareness of the environmental consequences of single-use plastics has grown, there has been a renewed focus on sustainable materials and practices. Many companies now offer eco-friendly coffee mugs made from recycled materials or renewable resources. Additionally, the popularity of reusable coffee mugs has surged, with many people opting to bring their own mugs to coffee shops to reduce waste.

The cultural significance of the coffee mug cannot be overstated. In many ways, it is more than just a vessel for holding a beverage; it is a symbol of comfort, routine, and personal expression. For many people, the ritual of drinking coffee from a favorite mug is an important part of their daily routine. Coffee mugs can also hold sentimental value, often associated with memories of places visited, gifts received, or milestones celebrated.

Chapter 12: The Rise of the Wristwatch

The rise of the wristwatch is a fascinating narrative that spans centuries, encapsulating advancements in technology, shifts in societal norms, and changes in aesthetic preferences. The wristwatch, a ubiquitous accessory in contemporary life, has evolved from a symbol of status and wealth to an essential tool for timekeeping and fashion.

The history of timekeeping dates back to ancient civilizations, which used sundials, water clocks, and other rudimentary devices to measure time. The advent of mechanical clocks in the 14th century marked a significant leap forward, but these early clocks were large and cumbersome, often found in church towers and public spaces. Personal timekeeping devices, like the portable clocks developed in the 15th century, began to emerge, but they were still far from the wristwatches we know today.

The earliest portable timepieces were pocket watches, which gained popularity in the 16th century. These early watches were intricate and expensive, often worn as a status symbol by the wealthy. They were usually carried in pockets or attached to clothing with chains. The first known wristwatches, however, were created in the late 16th century, and they were predominantly worn by women as decorative items. These early wristwatches were often considered more as jewelry than practical timekeeping devices.

The 19th century brought significant advancements in watchmaking technology, particularly with the development of the lever escapement, which improved accuracy and reliability. The introduction of mass production techniques by companies like Waltham Watch Company and Elgin National Watch Company in the United States made watches more affordable and accessible. Despite these advancements, wristwatches remained relatively uncommon compared to pocket watches, which were still the preferred choice for men.

The transition from pocket watches to wristwatches was accelerated by military needs. During the Boer War (1899-1902) and World War I (1914-1918), soldiers found wristwatches to be far more practical than pocket watches. The necessity for synchronized maneuvers and coordinated attacks made accurate timekeeping essential, and the ease of checking a wristwatch under combat conditions proved invaluable. These military wristwatches were often equipped with luminous dials and sturdy straps, features that would become standard in later models.

The post-World War I era saw wristwatches gaining widespread popularity among civilians. The interwar period was marked by a shift in fashion and societal norms, with men increasingly adopting wristwatches as a practical and stylish accessory. Watchmakers capitalized on this trend by producing a wide range of designs, catering to different tastes and preferences. Iconic brands such as Rolex, founded in 1905, played a significant role in popularizing the wristwatch, introducing innovations like the first waterproof watch, the Rolex Oyster, in 1926.

The 20th century was a period of rapid technological advancement in watchmaking. The development of the quartz movement in the 1960s revolutionized the industry. Quartz watches, which use a battery-powered oscillator to regulate timekeeping, offered unprecedented accuracy and affordability. The introduction of quartz watches by Seiko in 1969, with their Astron model, marked the beginning of the "Quartz Revolution," which dramatically reduced the cost of watches and made them accessible to a broader audience.

The rise of digital technology in the 1970s and 1980s brought further innovations to the wristwatch. Digital watches, which display time using LED or LCD screens, became popular for their precision and modern look. Companies like Casio and Timex led the way in producing digital watches that were not only functional but also fashionable. Features like alarms, timers, and calculators added to the appeal, making digital watches a symbol of the era's technological progress.

Despite the dominance of quartz and digital watches, mechanical watches continued to hold a place of prestige and admiration. The craftsmanship and intricate engineering of mechanical movements, especially those of high-end brands like Patek Philippe, Audemars Piguet, and Vacheron Constantin, maintained a loyal following among watch enthusiasts and collectors. The late 20th century saw a resurgence of interest in mechanical watches, driven by a growing appreciation for traditional watchmaking skills and the artistry involved in creating these timepieces.

The advent of the 21st century introduced new dimensions to wristwatches with the emergence of smartwatches. These devices, which integrate timekeeping with digital functionality, have transformed the wristwatch into a multifunctional gadget. The launch of the Apple Watch in 2015 marked a significant milestone, offering features such as fitness tracking, notifications, and connectivity with other smart devices. Smartwatches have continued to evolve, incorporating advanced health monitoring capabilities, GPS, and even cellular connectivity, blurring the lines between traditional wristwatches and modern technology.

The rise of the wristwatch is also a story of design evolution. From the ornate and delicate designs of early wristwatches to the rugged and functional styles of military watches, the aesthetics of wristwatches have continuously adapted to changing tastes and cultural influences. The mid-20th century, in particular, saw the emergence of iconic designs that remain influential today. The Rolex Submariner, introduced in 1953, set the standard for dive watches with its robust construction and distinctive look. Similarly, the Omega Speedmaster, famously worn by NASA astronauts during the Apollo missions, became a symbol of precision and reliability.

The fashion industry has also played a crucial role in the evolution of wristwatch design. Luxury fashion brands such as Chanel, Gucci, and Louis Vuitton entered the watch market, bringing a new emphasis on style and brand identity. Collaborations between watchmakers and fashion designers have resulted in innovative and eye-catching designs, appealing to a diverse and fashion-conscious audience.

In recent years, sustainability has become an important consideration in the watch industry. Consumers are increasingly aware of the environmental impact of manufacturing processes and the ethical sourcing of materials. In response, many watch brands have adopted sustainable practices, such as using recycled materials, implementing eco-friendly production methods, and ensuring fair labor practices. This shift reflects a broader trend towards sustainability in the fashion and luxury goods sectors.

The cultural significance of wristwatches cannot be overstated. They have been symbols of status, tools of precision, and expressions of personal style. The gifting of wristwatches often carries sentimental value, marking significant life events such as graduations, anniversaries, and retirements. Collectors and enthusiasts form vibrant communities, sharing their passion for horology through forums, clubs, and exhibitions. The wristwatch, despite its small size, encapsulates a rich tapestry of human history, innovation, and culture.

The future of wristwatches is likely to be shaped by continued technological advancements and evolving consumer preferences. As smartwatches become more sophisticated, offering features that were once the realm of science fiction, traditional wristwatches will continue to hold their own, cherished for their craftsmanship, heritage, and timeless appeal. The integration of new materials, such as advanced ceramics and sustainable options, will further diversify the market.

Moreover, the rise of personalized and bespoke watchmaking services reflects a growing desire for individuality and uniqueness in a mass-produced world. Customization options, from engraving to choosing specific components and materials, allow consumers to create wristwatches that reflect their personal style and values.

Chapter 13: The Creation of the Velcro Fastener

The creation of the Velcro fastener is a remarkable story of innovation and inspiration, drawing from the natural world to solve practical problems. Velcro, a portmanteau of the French words "velours" (velvet) and "crochet" (hook), is a hook-and-loop fastener system that has revolutionized various industries since its invention in the mid-20th century. The journey of Velcro from a simple observation to a ubiquitous fastening solution involves a blend of curiosity, scientific research, and entrepreneurial spirit.

The origin of Velcro can be traced back to 1941, when Swiss engineer Georges de Mestral embarked on a hunting trip with his dog in the Alps. Upon returning home, he noticed that his clothing and his dog's fur were covered in burrs, the seed pods of burdock plants. Intrigued by their tenacity, de Mestral examined the burrs under a microscope and discovered that they were covered in tiny hooks that attached themselves to the loops in the fabric of his clothing. This simple observation sparked an idea: to create a man-made fastening system that mimicked this natural mechanism.

De Mestral faced numerous challenges in turning his idea into a practical product. He spent several years experimenting with different materials and manufacturing techniques. Early attempts involved cotton, which proved to be unsuitable due to its tendency to break and wear out quickly. De Mestral then turned to synthetic fibers, which offered greater durability and strength. He eventually settled on nylon, a material that had been developed by DuPont in the 1930s and was known for its resilience and elasticity.

Creating the hook-and-loop system required innovative manufacturing techniques. De Mestral worked with weavers to develop a method for producing the hooks, which involved weaving nylon into loops and then cutting the tops of the loops to create hooks. For the loop side of the fastener, he used uncut nylon loops. Achieving the right balance of strength and flexibility was critical, and de Mestral faced many setbacks in the process. Despite these challenges, he persisted, driven by his belief in the potential of his invention.

In 1955, after nearly a decade of research and development, de Mestral received a patent for his hook-and-loop fastener. He named his invention Velcro, combining the French words for velvet and hook. The initial reception of Velcro was lukewarm, as the material and the concept were unfamiliar to many. However, de Mestral's persistence and vision gradually paid off as he began to find applications for Velcro in various industries.

One of the first major breakthroughs for Velcro came in the aerospace industry. In the early 1960s, NASA recognized the potential of Velcro for use in space missions. The Apollo astronauts needed a reliable fastening system for their suits, equipment, and other items in the zero-gravity environment of space. Velcro proved to be an ideal solution due to its simplicity, reliability, and ease of use. NASA's adoption of Velcro brought significant attention and credibility to the fastener, leading to wider acceptance and use in other fields.

As Velcro gained popularity, it began to be used in a wide range of applications. In the fashion industry, Velcro became a convenient alternative to buttons, zippers, and laces. It was particularly useful for children's clothing and shoes, where ease of use and safety were important considerations. In the medical field, Velcro was used for orthopedic devices, bandages, and other medical equipment that required adjustable and secure fastening. The sports industry also embraced Velcro for athletic shoes, gloves, and other gear that benefited from quick and adjustable closures.

The versatility of Velcro continued to drive its adoption across various sectors. In the automotive industry, it was used for securing floor mats, seat covers, and other interior components. The military found applications for Velcro in uniforms, gear, and equipment, where its durability and ease of use were highly valued. In the consumer electronics market, Velcro was used to manage cables and secure devices. The construction industry utilized Velcro for temporary fastening solutions and tool organization.

Despite its widespread success, Velcro has faced challenges and competition over the years. The expiration of de Mestral's original patent in the late 1970s opened the market to other manufacturers, leading to the development of similar hook-and-loop fasteners. These competitors, often referred to as "generic Velcro," offered alternatives at different price points and quality levels. To maintain its market position, Velcro Industries, the company founded by de Mestral, continued to innovate and improve its products.

One significant area of innovation for Velcro Industries has been the development of new materials and designs. The company has introduced high-performance versions of Velcro that offer increased strength, durability, and resistance to extreme conditions. These advancements have expanded the use of Velcro in demanding environments such as aerospace, military, and industrial applications. Velcro Industries has also focused on improving the aesthetics of its fasteners, offering a wider range of colors and textures to meet the needs of fashion and consumer products.

In addition to material innovations, Velcro Industries has invested in sustainable practices and products. Recognizing the growing importance of environmental responsibility, the company has developed eco-friendly versions of its fasteners made from recycled materials. These products aim to reduce the environmental impact of Velcro production and meet the increasing demand for sustainable solutions in various industries.

The story of Velcro's rise to prominence is also a testament to effective branding and marketing. The name "Velcro" has become synonymous with hook-and-loop fasteners, much like "Kleenex" for tissues or "Xerox" for photocopying. Velcro Industries has leveraged this brand recognition through strategic marketing campaigns and partnerships. The company has emphasized the versatility, reliability, and ease of use of its products, appealing to both consumers and businesses.

The cultural impact of Velcro is evident in its widespread use and recognition. Velcro has become a part of everyday language, often used as a verb ("to Velcro something") or an adjective ("Velcro shoes"). Its presence in popular culture, from children's toys to high fashion, reflects its integration into daily life. The simplicity and effectiveness of Velcro have made it a symbol of ingenuity and practicality.

Chapter 14: The Mystery of the Scissors

The mystery of the scissors, an essential tool with a fascinating history, spans thousands of years and touches on various aspects of human civilization, technology, and culture. Scissors, in their simplest form, are hand-operated cutting instruments consisting of two blades that pivot at a central point. The evolution of these blades, from rudimentary shears to the highly specialized tools we use today, reflects advancements in metallurgy, design, and usage.

The earliest known scissors-like tools date back to around 3,000-1,500 BCE in ancient Egypt. These early scissors were made from bronze and operated on a spring mechanism, where the two blades were connected at the handle end, and the cutting action was achieved by squeezing the blades together. The tension of the bronze would return the blades to an open position. These primitive scissors were primarily used for cutting hair and other relatively soft materials.

Scissors in ancient Rome around 100 AD took a more familiar form with pivoted blades. Roman scissors were constructed from bronze or iron and featured a design where the blades pivoted at a point between the handles and the cutting tips. This design provided better leverage and made cutting more efficient, leading to wider usage for various tasks, including textile work, personal grooming, and even medical applications. The Romans' use of more durable materials like iron also contributed to the longevity and functionality of these early scissors.

The Middle Ages saw further refinement in the design and manufacture of scissors. As blacksmithing and metalworking techniques advanced, scissors became more durable and efficient. By the 14th century, scissors had become a common tool in Europe, used by tailors, barbers, and craftsmen. During this period, scissors were typically custom-made by blacksmiths, with each pair reflecting the individual craftsmanship of its maker. The design remained relatively consistent, with the pivot point closer to the blades than the handles, maximizing the cutting power.

The Industrial Revolution in the 18th and 19th centuries brought significant changes to the production of scissors. The advent of mass production techniques and advancements in metallurgy made it possible to produce scissors on a larger scale with more consistent quality. Factories in England, Germany, and the United States began producing scissors in large quantities, making them more accessible to the general public. Sheffield, England, became particularly renowned for its high-quality scissors, benefiting from the city's expertise in steel production.

One of the key innovations during this period was the introduction of cast steel, which improved the hardness and durability of scissor blades. The Bessemer process, developed in the mid-19th century, allowed for the mass production of high-quality steel, which in turn made scissors stronger and more affordable. Additionally, the development of precise machining techniques enabled the production of scissors with uniform blade alignment and cutting edges, enhancing their performance and reliability.

The 20th century saw further diversification and specialization in the types of scissors available. Scissors were designed for specific tasks and industries, leading to a wide variety of forms and functions. For instance, sewing scissors and fabric shears featured long blades for cutting through textiles, while pinking shears were designed with serrated blades to create a zigzag edge that prevented fabric from fraying. Medical scissors, such as surgical scissors and bandage scissors, were crafted with precision and hygiene in mind, often featuring stainless steel for its corrosion-resistant properties.

One notable advancement in scissor design during the 20th century was the development of ergonomic handles. Traditional scissors often caused discomfort with prolonged use, especially for professionals like tailors and seamstresses. Manufacturers began experimenting with handle shapes and materials to improve comfort and reduce hand fatigue. Innovations such as molded plastic handles, finger rests, and spring-loaded mechanisms were introduced, making scissors more user-friendly and efficient.

The advent of modern materials and technologies also played a significant role in the evolution of scissors. The use of stainless steel became widespread, offering superior corrosion resistance and durability. Additionally, the development of synthetic materials like plastic allowed for lightweight, durable handles that could be molded into ergonomic shapes. Coatings such as titanium and Teflon were applied to blades to enhance cutting performance and reduce friction.

Scissors have also found their place in art and culture. The craft of scissor-making has been celebrated in various forms, from intricate, hand-forged Japanese scissors known as nigiri basami, used in traditional textile arts, to the ornate embroidery scissors from Europe. These specialized tools are often regarded as works of art in their own right, showcasing the skill and creativity of their makers.

The cultural significance of scissors extends beyond their practical applications. In many cultures, scissors are imbued with symbolic meanings and superstitions. In ancient China, scissors were often included in wedding dowries as symbols of unity and fidelity. Similarly, in some European traditions, giving scissors as a gift was believed to bring bad luck unless a coin was exchanged to "pay" for them, thus neutralizing the potential ill fortune.

Scissors have also appeared in literature, folklore, and art. They have been used as metaphors for cutting ties or severing relationships and have featured in various myths and stories. For example, the Greek myth of Atropos, one of the three Fates, depicts her as using scissors to cut the thread of life, determining an individual's moment of death. This imagery highlights the powerful and sometimes ominous symbolism associated with scissors.

In the modern era, scissors continue to be indispensable tools in numerous fields. In the fashion industry, they remain essential for cutting fabrics and finishing garments. In the culinary world, kitchen scissors are used for tasks ranging from snipping herbs to trimming meat. In the medical field, surgical scissors are critical instruments for precision cutting during operations. The versatility and utility of scissors ensure their continued relevance in a wide range of applications.

The mystery of the scissors also lies in their simplicity and effectiveness. Despite the myriad technological advancements and new tools developed over the centuries, the basic design of scissors has remained largely unchanged. This enduring design speaks to the fundamental efficiency of the tool. The concept of two blades pivoting to create a cutting action is elegantly simple yet incredibly effective, demonstrating the power of straightforward engineering solutions.

In recent years, there has been a renewed interest in high-quality, handcrafted scissors. Artisanal scissor makers around the world are preserving traditional techniques while also experimenting with new materials and designs. These craftsmen produce scissors that are not only functional but also aesthetically pleasing, often becoming cherished items passed down through generations.

Chapter 15: The Tale of the Toothpick

The tale of the toothpick is a fascinating journey that spans human history, reflecting changes in culture, technology, and hygiene practices. Toothpicks, simple tools used primarily for removing food particles from between teeth, have evolved from rudimentary natural implements to mass-produced items with a variety of designs and uses. This story encompasses ancient civilizations, royal courts, technological advancements, and modern consumer culture.

The history of the toothpick likely begins with the earliest humans. Primitive toothpicks were probably made from twigs, bird feathers, porcupine quills, or other small, pointed objects found in nature. Archaeological evidence suggests that Neanderthals and early Homo sapiens used toothpicks made from grass stalks or small bones. Fossilized remains of early humans often show wear marks on teeth that indicate the use of such tools to remove food debris or soothe gum irritations.

The use of toothpicks is documented in many ancient civilizations. In Mesopotamia, around 3000 BCE, toothpicks were made from precious metals like gold and silver, signifying their importance and the wealth of their owners. The ancient Egyptians, known for their meticulous personal hygiene practices, also used toothpicks, which were often included in burial tombs to ensure the deceased's continued dental care in the afterlife. Similarly, the ancient Greeks and Romans had a variety of toothpicks made from materials such as wood, metal, and bone. Roman literature and artifacts, including references in the writings of the poet Horace, indicate that toothpicks were a common and accepted part of daily life.

In the Middle Ages, the use of toothpicks continued in Europe and the Islamic world. Wealthy individuals often carried personal toothpicks made from precious metals, sometimes encrusted with jewels. These toothpicks were not just practical items but also symbols of status and sophistication. During this period, toothpicks were often carried in elaborate cases, reflecting the craftsmanship and artistry of the time. In the Islamic world, dental hygiene was highly valued, and toothpicks made from the twigs of the Salvadora persica tree, known as miswak, were widely used. Miswak twigs contain natural antibacterial properties and have been used for dental care for thousands of years, a practice that continues in some cultures today.

The Renaissance period saw an increased emphasis on personal hygiene and the use of toothpicks among the European elite. The French court, in particular, was known for its elaborate and ornate toothpicks made from gold and silver. These toothpicks often had intricate designs and were sometimes combined with other grooming tools. The use of toothpicks spread among the upper classes, becoming an essential accessory for nobles and wealthy merchants.

The mass production of toothpicks began in the 19th century, revolutionizing their availability and use. The story of modern toothpicks is closely linked to the entrepreneurial spirit of a man named Charles Forster. Forster, an American businessman, is credited with popularizing the mass production of toothpicks in the United States. In the mid-1800s, Forster traveled to Brazil, where he observed the use of toothpicks made from indigenous woods. Recognizing the potential market for such items in the U.S., he began importing Brazilian wood to produce toothpicks.

Forster faced initial resistance from American consumers, who were not accustomed to using manufactured toothpicks. To overcome this, he employed innovative marketing techniques, including hiring Harvard students to dine at restaurants and demand toothpicks after their meals. This created a perceived demand and encouraged restaurants to stock Forster's toothpicks. His efforts paid off, and by the late 1800s, Forster's toothpicks became widely popular across the United States.

The success of Forster's business led to the establishment of toothpick factories in Maine, which became the center of toothpick production in the United States. These factories utilized local birch wood, known for its strength and pliability, to produce toothpicks. The manufacturing process involved cutting logs into thin strips, which were then sharpened and polished to create uniform toothpicks. By the early 20th century, Maine was producing billions of toothpicks annually, making it the toothpick capital of the world.

The 20th century saw further innovations in toothpick design and production. The introduction of plastic toothpicks provided a durable and flexible alternative to wooden toothpicks. These plastic versions often featured added functionalities, such as textured surfaces for better cleaning and dual-ended designs with a pick on one end and a brush on the other. In addition to plastic, other materials such as bamboo and stainless steel were used to create reusable and eco-friendly toothpicks.

The design of toothpicks also evolved to include various shapes and features. The traditional round toothpick remained popular, but flat and triangular designs were introduced to improve effectiveness in removing food particles. Decorative toothpicks, often used for appetizers and cocktails, featured colorful or themed embellishments, adding a festive touch to social gatherings.

Toothpicks also found a place in popular culture and art. They have been featured in literature, films, and television shows, often symbolizing nonchalance or meticulous attention to detail. The iconic image of a character chewing on a toothpick, as seen in countless Westerns and gangster movies, has become a cultural trope. Additionally, artists and hobbyists have used toothpicks to create intricate sculptures and models, showcasing the versatility and creativity inspired by this simple tool.

In recent years, the environmental impact of single-use plastic items, including plastic toothpicks, has come under scrutiny. As a result, there has been a resurgence in the use of biodegradable materials such as wood and bamboo for toothpick production. Many companies now offer eco-friendly toothpicks that are sustainably sourced and compostable, aligning with growing consumer demand for environmentally responsible products.

The health benefits of using toothpicks, particularly those made from natural materials like miswak, have been the subject of scientific research. Studies have shown that miswak contains compounds with antimicrobial properties, which can help reduce plaque and prevent gum disease. This traditional practice of using natural toothpicks for dental hygiene continues to be supported by modern science, highlighting the enduring wisdom of ancient customs.

The tale of the toothpick also reflects broader trends in consumer behavior and societal values. The shift from handcrafted, personalized toothpicks to mass-produced, standardized products mirror the industrialization and commercialization of many aspects of daily life. The subsequent move towards sustainable and eco-friendly alternatives indicates a growing awareness of environmental issues and a desire to return to more natural and responsible practices.

Chapter 16: The Advent of the Safety Razor

The advent of the safety razor marks a significant milestone in the history of personal grooming, revolutionizing the way people shave and transforming a daily chore into a safer, more convenient, and more efficient process. The story of the safety razor involves innovation, entrepreneurship, and cultural shifts, reflecting changes in technology, hygiene practices, and consumer behavior over the centuries.

Before the invention of the safety razor, shaving was a precarious task primarily performed with straight razors, also known as cut-throat razors. These razors consisted of a single, sharp blade that could be folded into its handle when not in use. Straight razors required significant skill to use safely, as they could easily cause cuts, nicks, and serious injuries if not handled correctly. Consequently, many men either visited professional barbers for a shave or relied on their own ability, often resulting in a time-consuming and risky endeavor.

The origins of the safety razor can be traced back to the 18th and 19th centuries when various inventors sought to create a safer alternative to the straight razor. One of the earliest developments came in the late 18th century with the introduction of the "guard razor" in France. This rudimentary design featured a protective guard along the blade's edge to minimize the risk of cuts. However, the guard razor did not gain widespread popularity and was limited in its effectiveness.

The true breakthrough in safety razor design came in the mid-19th century with the work of a British inventor named William Henson. In 1847, Henson patented a new razor design that positioned the blade at a right angle to the handle, resembling the shape of a modern hoe. This design, often referred to as the "hoe razor," provided better control and safety compared to previous models. Although Henson's design was a significant improvement, it still required users to sharpen the blade regularly, which limited its practicality.

The next major advancement occurred in the late 19th century with the efforts of King Camp Gillette, an American businessman and inventor. Gillette's idea was to create a razor with a disposable blade, eliminating the need for sharpening and making shaving more convenient and accessible. In 1901, Gillette, along with MIT-trained machinist William Nickerson, developed the first safety razor with a double-edged, replaceable blade. The razor featured a protective guard that exposed only the very edge of the blade, reducing the risk of cuts and making it safer and easier to use than traditional straight razors.

Gillette's invention was revolutionary for several reasons. First, the disposable blade concept meant that users could always have a sharp blade without the hassle of honing and stropping. This made shaving quicker, more convenient, and accessible to a broader audience. Second, the design of the safety razor allowed for mass production, significantly reducing the cost of razors and blades. Gillette's business model focused on selling the razor handle at an affordable price while making a profit from the ongoing sale of disposable blades, a strategy that proved to be highly successful.

The introduction of Gillette's safety razor coincided with significant cultural and societal changes. At the turn of the 20th century, personal hygiene and grooming were becoming increasingly important in Western societies. The growing emphasis on cleanliness and appearance, particularly among the burgeoning middle class, created a receptive market for Gillette's innovative product. Additionally, the rise of advertising and mass media allowed Gillette to effectively market his razors to a wide audience, promoting the safety razor as a modern, convenient, and essential grooming tool.

The safety razor quickly gained popularity, and by the time of World War I, it had become a standard item for soldiers. The U.S. military issued Gillette safety razors to its troops, both for practical reasons and to maintain morale. Soldiers appreciated the convenience and safety of the razors, and many continued to use them after the war, further cementing the safety razor's place in American culture. Gillette's success continued to grow, and by the 1920s, the company had expanded internationally, establishing the safety razor as a global phenomenon.

The success of Gillette's safety razor inspired other companies to enter the market, leading to increased competition and innovation. Companies such as Schick, founded by Jacob Schick, introduced new designs and features to enhance the shaving experience. In 1928, Schick patented the first electric razor, which used a motor to oscillate the blades, providing a close shave without the need for water or shaving cream. Although electric razors would eventually carve out their own niche in the shaving market, they did not eclipse the popularity of safety razors.

Throughout the 20th century, the design and materials of safety razors continued to evolve. The introduction of stainless-steel blades in the 1960s improved durability and sharpness, reducing the frequency of blade changes. Plastic and metal handles became more ergonomic and aesthetically pleasing, catering to consumer preferences for comfort and style. The development of multi-blade razors in the late 20th century, such as the Gillette Mach3 introduced in 1998, further enhanced the shaving experience by providing a closer shave with fewer strokes, reducing skin irritation.

The marketing and branding strategies of razor companies also played a significant role in shaping consumer behavior. Companies invested heavily in advertising campaigns that emphasized the benefits of their products, such as a closer shave, smoother skin, and advanced technology. Celebrity endorsements, sponsorships, and promotional events helped to create brand loyalty and drive sales. The iconic tagline "The Best a Man Can Get," introduced by Gillette in 1989, became synonymous with quality and performance, reinforcing the brand's dominance in the market.

In addition to advancements in blade technology and design, the safety razor industry has also responded to changing social norms and gender dynamics. Initially marketed primarily to men, safety razors began to be targeted at women in the mid-20th century. Companies introduced razors specifically designed for women, with features such as curved handles and softer grips to accommodate shaving legs and underarms. Advertising campaigns highlighted the benefits of smooth, hair-free skin, aligning with evolving beauty standards and expanding the market for safety razors.

The environmental impact of disposable razor blades has become a growing concern in recent years, leading to a resurgence of interest in traditional safety razors with reusable handles and recyclable blades. This shift is part of a broader movement towards sustainable consumer products, as individuals seek to reduce waste and make more environmentally conscious choices. Companies have responded by offering eco-friendly options, such as razors made from sustainable materials and blade recycling programs.

The advent of the internet and e-commerce has further transformed the safety razor market. Online retailers and subscription services have made it easier than ever for consumers to purchase razors and blades, often at competitive prices. Direct-to-consumer brands like Dollar Shave Club and Harry's have disrupted the traditional razor market by offering convenient, cost-effective alternatives to established brands, leveraging digital marketing and subscription models to attract and retain customers.

Chapter 17: The Creation of the Hand Sanitizer

The creation of hand sanitizer is an intriguing tale that intertwines scientific discovery, public health, and societal needs. It is a journey that begins with the foundational understanding of germs and hygiene, leading to an indispensable product that has become a staple in daily life, especially underscored during global health crises such as the COVID-19 pandemic.

The concept of sanitizing hands dates back to the 19th century when Ignaz Semmelweis, a Hungarian physician, demonstrated that handwashing with chlorinated lime solutions could drastically reduce the incidence of puerperal fever in obstetric clinics. Semmelweis's work laid the groundwork for understanding the critical role of hand hygiene in preventing infections. However, it wasn't until the late 20th century that hand sanitizer as we know it began to take shape.

The journey to modern hand sanitizers began in the healthcare industry. In the 1960s, hospitals and clinics sought effective ways to reduce the spread of pathogens, particularly in settings where soap and water were not always readily available. Traditional handwashing, though effective, was time-consuming and not always feasible in fast-paced medical environments. This need spurred the search for alternative solutions that could provide similar levels of hygiene without the need for water.

The key breakthrough came with the development of alcohol-based hand sanitizers. Alcohol, specifically ethanol or isopropanol, is an excellent antimicrobial agent that can effectively kill a broad spectrum of bacteria and viruses. In 1966, Lupe Hernandez, a nursing student from Bakersfield, California, is often credited with inventing the modern hand sanitizer. She conceptualized a gel-based formula that could be used to disinfect hands without the need for soap and water.

This idea was revolutionary, providing a portable, quick, and effective means of maintaining hand hygiene.

The formulation of hand sanitizers typically includes alcohol concentrations ranging from 60% to 95%, combined with water and other ingredients such as glycerin or aloe vera to prevent skin dryness and provide a soothing effect. The high alcohol content is crucial, as it disrupts the protein and lipid structures of microbes, leading to their rapid inactivation and death. The addition of moisturizing agents addresses a common concern with alcohol-based products: the potential for skin irritation and dryness with frequent use.

Hand sanitizers gained popularity initially within the healthcare sector. Medical professionals found them to be an invaluable tool for maintaining hygiene in environments where immediate access to soap and water was limited. The convenience and efficacy of these products soon extended beyond hospitals, finding a place in public spaces, offices, schools, and homes.

The 1980s and 1990s saw a gradual increase in the commercial availability of hand sanitizers. Companies began marketing them to the general public, emphasizing their ease of use and effectiveness in killing germs. These products were particularly appealing to parents, travelers, and anyone looking to maintain hand hygiene on the go. The portability of hand sanitizers, often packaged in small bottles or dispensers, made them a practical addition to purses, backpacks, and desks.

A significant turning point in the widespread acceptance of hand sanitizers came with the H1N1 influenza pandemic in 2009. This global health crisis heightened public awareness of the importance of hand hygiene in preventing the spread of infectious diseases. Sales of hand sanitizers soared as people sought ways to protect themselves and their families from the virus. Public health campaigns and guidelines from organizations such as the World Health Organization (WHO) and the Centers for Disease Control and Prevention (CDC) further reinforced the importance of hand sanitizers as part of a comprehensive approach to hygiene.

The COVID-19 pandemic, beginning in late 2019, brought hand sanitizers to the forefront of global consciousness. As the novel coronavirus spread rapidly around the world, hand sanitizers became a critical tool in the fight against the virus. Governments, health organizations, and businesses emphasized their use as a key measure to reduce transmission. This unprecedented demand led to shortages and prompted many companies, including distilleries and cosmetic manufacturers, to pivot their production lines to produce hand sanitizers. The pandemic also spurred innovation in hand sanitizer formulations, with companies exploring new ingredients and delivery systems to improve efficacy and user experience.

Beyond their role in preventing infectious diseases, hand sanitizers have also found applications in various other contexts. In food service industries, they help maintain hygiene standards and prevent cross-contamination. In schools and childcare settings, they provide a convenient way to ensure that children and staff can maintain clean hands, especially in situations where handwashing facilities may be limited. Even in everyday situations, such as shopping or commuting, hand sanitizers offer a quick and effective means of reducing the risk of microbial contamination.

Chapter 18: The History of the Stapler

The history of the stapler is a fascinating journey that spans several centuries, tracing the evolution of a simple yet indispensable tool that has revolutionized how we organize and manage paper documents. From its rudimentary beginnings to the sophisticated devices we use today, the stapler's development is a testament to human ingenuity and the continuous quest for efficiency in office work and personal organization.

The origins of the stapler can be traced back to the 18th century, specifically to the reign of King Louis XV of France. It is widely believed that the first stapler was crafted for the king himself, as he required a device to fasten documents together securely. This early stapler was an ornate, hand-crafted tool, made from precious metals and adorned with intricate designs. Each staple used in this device was handmade and inscribed with the royal insignia, underscoring its exclusive nature and the high status of its user. While this early version of the stapler was far from practical for widespread use, it marked the beginning of the quest for a reliable paper fastening solution.

The 19th century brought significant advancements in stapling technology, driven by the industrial revolution and the consequent surge in administrative work and document management. In 1841, Samuel Slocum, an American inventor, patented a device for sticking pins into paper. Although not a stapler by modern standards, Slocum's invention laid the groundwork for the development of more efficient paper fastening tools. His device was primarily used to attach pins to paper labels, which were then applied to fabrics, demonstrating an early attempt to mechanize the process of attaching items to paper.

The real breakthrough in stapler technology came in 1866, when George McGill, another American inventor, patented a small, bendable brass paper fastener. McGill's invention was simple yet effective: a small metal clip that could bind several sheets of paper together. This was followed by his patent for a press that inserted the fastener into the paper, which was the precursor to the modern stapler. McGill's device was revolutionary because it combined the fastener and the mechanism to insert it, paving the way for the development of an all-in-one stapling tool.

The first commercially successful stapler, often referred to as the "Novelty Paper Fastener," was introduced by McGill in 1879. This device could hold a single staple at a time and was operated manually. Users had to insert a staple into the stapler, position the paper, and press the lever to drive the staple through the paper. While cumbersome by today's standards, McGill's stapler was a significant improvement over previous methods and quickly gained popularity in offices and businesses.

As the demand for more efficient stapling solutions grew, inventors and manufacturers continued to refine and improve the design. In 1895, the E.H. Hotchkiss Company introduced the "No. 1 Paper Fastener," a stapler that could hold multiple staples at once and featured a spring-loaded mechanism to advance the next staple into position. This innovation greatly increased the speed and convenience of stapling, making it more practical for everyday use.

The early 20th century saw further innovations in stapler design, driven by the increasing complexity of office work and the need for more efficient document management. In 1937, the Boston Wire Stitcher Company, later known as Bostitch, introduced the "Bostitch Model B5," a stapler that could hold a strip of staples and featured a mechanism to cut and crimp the wire staples. This design became the standard for modern staplers, offering a significant improvement in ease of use and reliability.

The introduction of the stapler into offices and schools revolutionized the way people handled documents. It provided a simple, reliable means of binding multiple sheets of paper together, reducing the need for bulky and time-consuming methods such as sewing or using pins. Staplers quickly became an essential tool in the office, helping to streamline administrative tasks and improve organizational efficiency.

Staplers have continued to evolve over the decades, with manufacturers introducing new features and improvements to meet the changing needs of users. In the 1950s and 1960s, electric staplers were developed, providing a faster and more efficient means of stapling large volumes of paper. These devices used electric motors to drive the staples, eliminating the need for manual effort and greatly increasing the speed of the stapling process.

In addition to electric staplers, other specialized staplers were developed to address specific needs. Heavy-duty staplers, capable of binding thick stacks of paper, became popular in industries that required the organization of large documents. Stapleless staplers, which cut and fold paper to bind it together without the use of metal staples, were introduced as an environmentally friendly alternative. These innovations expanded the versatility and functionality of staplers, making them indispensable tools in a wide range of settings.

The materials used in staplers have also evolved over time. Early staplers were made from metal, but advancements in materials science have led to the development of staplers made from lightweight and durable plastics. These modern staplers are not only more affordable but also more ergonomic, featuring designs that reduce hand strain and improve user comfort.

In the digital age, the role of the stapler has adapted to the changing landscape of document management. While the proliferation of digital documents and paperless offices has reduced the reliance on physical paper, staplers remain a vital tool for situations where hard copies are necessary. Legal documents, contracts, and educational materials are just a few examples of items that still require physical binding, ensuring the continued relevance of staplers in the modern world.

The stapler has also found its way into popular culture, becoming a symbol of office life and productivity. The red Swingline stapler, famously featured in the 1999 film "Office Space," has become an iconic image, representing the everyday struggles and triumphs of office workers. This cultural significance underscores the stapler's enduring presence in our lives, even as the tools and technologies we use continue to evolve.

Chapter 19: The Discovery of the Microwave Oven

The discovery of the microwave oven is a remarkable story of scientific serendipity, technological innovation, and the transformation of daily life. The microwave oven, now a common household appliance, revolutionized how we cook and heat food, providing unparalleled convenience and efficiency.

The story of the microwave oven begins during World War II, with the development of radar technology. Radar, an acronym for Radio Detection and Ranging, was crucial for military operations, allowing for the detection of enemy aircraft and ships. One of the key components of radar technology was the magnetron, a device that generates microwaves. These microwaves are electromagnetic waves with a frequency higher than that of radio waves but lower than that of infrared radiation. The magnetron was capable of producing high-powered microwaves, which were essential for the effective functioning of radar systems.

The serendipitous discovery of the microwave oven occurred in 1945, thanks to the curiosity and observational skills of Percy Spencer, an engineer working for Raytheon, a defense contractor involved in the development of radar technology. Spencer, who had no formal education beyond elementary school, was a self-taught engineer with an innate understanding of complex electrical systems. While working on an active radar set, Spencer noticed something unusual: a candy bar in his pocket had melted. Intrigued by this unexpected phenomenon, he began to experiment further.

Spencer placed popcorn kernels near the magnetron, and to his amazement, they began to pop. He then tried placing an egg near the device, which resulted in the egg exploding. These experiments led Spencer to conclude that the microwaves generated by the magnetron were causing the food to heat up rapidly. He realized that this accidental discovery had the potential to revolutionize cooking, as microwaves could heat food much faster than conventional methods.

Raytheon, recognizing the potential of Spencer's discovery, quickly moved to develop a commercial application for the technology. In 1947, the company introduced the first microwave oven, known as the "Radarange." This initial model was large, expensive, and primarily intended for use in commercial kitchens and restaurants. It stood nearly six feet tall, weighed over 750 pounds, and cost around $5,000, which was prohibitively expensive for most households. Despite these limitations, the Radarange demonstrated the feasibility and potential of microwave cooking, laying the groundwork for future innovations.

The early microwave ovens used water-cooled magnetrons and required significant power to operate. These initial models were not practical for widespread consumer use, but they served as important prototypes that allowed engineers to refine the technology. Throughout the 1950s and 1960s, improvements in magnetron design, materials, and manufacturing processes led to smaller, more efficient, and more affordable microwave ovens.

One of the significant breakthroughs in the development of the microwave oven was the transition from water-cooled to air-cooled magnetrons. This innovation significantly reduced the size and complexity of the ovens, making them more suitable for home use. Additionally, advances in electronics and manufacturing techniques allowed for the production of more reliable and cost-effective components.

The first commercially successful microwave oven for home use was introduced in 1967 by the Amana Corporation, a subsidiary of Raytheon. The Amana Radarange was a countertop model that retailed for around $495, making it more accessible to the average consumer. This model featured a more compact design, user-friendly controls, and improved safety features, such as a door that prevented the microwave from operating unless securely closed.

The introduction of the Amana Radarange marked a turning point in the history of the microwave oven. Throughout the 1970s and 1980s, microwave ovens gained popularity as manufacturers continued to improve their design, functionality, and affordability. By the late 1970s, the price of a microwave oven had dropped significantly, making it an attractive option for many households. The convenience of microwave cooking, coupled with aggressive marketing campaigns and demonstrations, helped to drive widespread adoption.

As microwave ovens became more prevalent, they also began to transform culinary practices and household routines. The ability to cook and reheat food quickly and efficiently revolutionized meal preparation, making it easier for busy families and working individuals to manage their time. Microwave ovens also facilitated the development of a new market for pre-packaged, microwaveable foods, further enhancing their appeal.

One of the key factors in the widespread acceptance of microwave ovens was the development of microwave-safe cookware and packaging. Early users of microwave ovens quickly discovered that not all materials were suitable for microwave cooking. Metal containers, for example, could cause sparks and fires, while certain plastics could melt or release harmful chemicals. In response, manufacturers developed a range of microwave-safe products, including glass, ceramic, and specially designed plastics, that could withstand the high temperatures and electromagnetic radiation generated by microwave ovens.

The impact of the microwave oven on society extends beyond the kitchen. In addition to revolutionizing home cooking, microwave technology has found applications in various fields, including medicine, telecommunications, and industrial processes. Microwave heating is used in medical treatments, such as diathermy and hyperthermia therapy, to treat certain conditions and diseases. In telecommunications, microwaves are used for wireless communication, including satellite and mobile phone signals. In industrial processes, microwave heating is employed for tasks such as drying, curing, and material processing.

Despite its many benefits, the microwave oven has also faced criticism and concerns over the years. Some people have raised questions about the safety of microwave radiation and its potential health effects. However, extensive research and regulatory oversight have shown that microwave ovens are safe when used according to the manufacturer's instructions. Microwave ovens are designed with multiple safety features, including shielding and interlock mechanisms, to prevent exposure to harmful levels of radiation.

Another area of concern has been the nutritional impact of microwave cooking. Critics have argued that microwaving food could lead to nutrient loss or the formation of harmful compounds. However, studies have shown that microwave cooking can actually preserve nutrients better than some traditional cooking methods, such as boiling, which can leach vitamins and minerals into the cooking water. The key to retaining nutrients in microwave cooking, as with any cooking method, is to avoid overcooking and to use minimal water.

The evolution of the microwave oven has continued into the 21st century, with new features and technologies enhancing its functionality and user experience. Modern microwave ovens often come with advanced capabilities, such as convection cooking, grilling, and sensor-based cooking programs that automatically adjust cooking time and power levels. These innovations have further expanded the versatility of microwave ovens, making them an even more valuable tool in the kitchen.

The environmental impact of microwave ovens has also been a topic of discussion. While microwave ovens are energy-efficient compared to traditional ovens and stovetops, their widespread use and the production of microwave-safe packaging have raised concerns about resource consumption and waste. Manufacturers and consumers alike are increasingly focused on sustainability, leading to efforts to reduce energy consumption, improve recyclability, and minimize the environmental footprint of microwave ovens and related products.

The discovery of the microwave oven is a remarkable example of how an accidental observation can lead to a technological revolution. Percy Spencer's curiosity and ingenuity turned a wartime innovation into a household staple that has transformed the way we cook and live. The microwave oven's journey from a bulky, expensive prototype to a ubiquitous kitchen appliance highlights the importance of continuous improvement, adaptation, and innovation.

Chapter 20: The Emergence of the Electric Fan

The emergence of the electric fan is a story that spans centuries and continents, involving a series of inventions, innovations, and adaptations that collectively transformed how we experience comfort in warm climates. The electric fan, a ubiquitous household and office appliance today, has its roots in ancient civilizations and has evolved through various technological advancements to become an indispensable part of modern life.

The concept of using artificial means to create airflow dates back to ancient civilizations. The earliest known fans were handheld and used manually to create a cooling breeze. These fans were made from materials such as feathers, palm leaves, and fabric, and were often used by the elite and royalty to maintain comfort in hot weather. In ancient Egypt, fans were depicted in tomb paintings, highlighting their significance in daily life and ceremonies. Similarly, in ancient China and India, fans were crafted from bamboo and silk, showcasing intricate designs and craftsmanship.

The first significant step towards mechanized fans came in the 1st century AD, with the invention of the rotary fan by the Chinese inventor Ding Huan. His fan was powered by a hand-cranked mechanism and used to ventilate buildings. This early fan design consisted of a series of interconnected wheels that rotated when cranked, creating a flow of air. This innovation was primarily used in palaces and large buildings to provide ventilation and cooling.

During the Renaissance period, Leonardo da Vinci conceptualized a mechanical fan. Da Vinci's design, although not realized in his lifetime, demonstrated an early understanding of the principles of air movement and mechanical power. His sketches included a device with a series of blades that rotated when powered by a foot pedal, much like a modern pedal-powered fan. While Da Vinci's fan never came to fruition, his ideas influenced future inventors and engineers.

The 18th and 19th centuries saw significant advancements in technology and engineering, setting the stage for the development of the electric fan. The Industrial Revolution brought about a wave of innovations in machinery and power sources, including the advent of steam engines and electric motors. These technological advancements laid the groundwork for the creation of electrically powered appliances.

The first practical electric fan was invented in the early 1880s by Schuyler Skaats Wheeler, an American engineer. Wheeler's fan used an electric motor to drive a set of blades, creating a steady flow of air. This early fan was relatively simple in design, consisting of a motor, a set of blades, and a protective cage. The fan was marketed by the Crocker & Curtis Electric Motor Company, where Wheeler worked, and was initially used in industrial and commercial settings to provide ventilation and cooling.

Around the same time, Philip Diehl, a German-American inventor, made significant contributions to the development of the electric fan. Diehl, who had previously worked on the development of electric lighting, applied his knowledge of electric motors to create the first ceiling fan in 1882. His design featured an electric motor mounted directly on the ceiling, with blades attached to the motor shaft. Diehl's ceiling fan was a major innovation, as it provided a more efficient and space-saving solution for cooling large rooms and buildings.

The widespread adoption of electric fans was initially limited by the availability of electricity. In the late 19th and early 20th centuries, electricity was not yet widespread, and many households and businesses did not have access to a reliable power source. However, as electrical infrastructure expanded and electricity became more accessible, the demand for electric fans grew. The development of alternating current (AC) by Nikola Tesla and the subsequent adoption of AC power systems played a crucial role in making electric fans more practical and widespread.

The early 20th century saw significant improvements in fan design and manufacturing. Companies such as General Electric, Westinghouse, and Emerson Electric began mass-producing electric fans, making them more affordable and accessible to the general public. These early electric fans were typically made of metal and featured robust construction, with heavy bases and sturdy blades. The designs varied, with some fans being oscillating, allowing them to rotate back and forth to cover a larger area, while others were stationary.

In the 1920s and 1930s, further advancements in materials and manufacturing techniques led to the development of lighter and more efficient fans. The introduction of die-cast aluminum allowed for the production of more lightweight and durable fan blades, while improvements in electric motor design made fans more efficient and quieter. The Art Deco movement of the 1920s also influenced fan design, with manufacturers creating fans that were not only functional but also aesthetically pleasing.

The post-World War II era marked a significant turning point in the history of the electric fan. The economic boom and the rise of the middle class led to increased consumer demand for household appliances, including electric fans. The development of plastic materials allowed for the production of more affordable and versatile fans. Plastic blades and housings made fans lighter, safer, and more accessible to a wider range of consumers. The 1950s and 1960s saw a proliferation of fan designs, with manufacturers offering a variety of styles, sizes, and features to suit different needs and preferences.

One of the major innovations in electric fan technology during this period was the introduction of the box fan. Box fans featured a rectangular housing with a large fan blade inside, providing a powerful and efficient cooling solution. These fans were designed to fit into windows or be placed on the floor, allowing for versatile use in different settings. Box fans became popular in homes and offices, providing an affordable and effective way to cool large areas.

In the latter half of the 20th century, advancements in electronics and automation led to the development of more sophisticated and feature-rich electric fans. Fans with variable speed controls, timers, and remote controls became common, offering greater convenience and customization. The introduction of bladeless fans by companies like Dyson in the early 21st century marked another significant innovation. These fans use air multiplier technology to create a smooth, powerful airflow without the use of traditional blades, providing a safer and more aesthetically pleasing alternative to conventional fans.

The emergence of the electric fan has also had a significant impact on global health and productivity. In many parts of the world, particularly in tropical and subtropical regions, electric fans have played a crucial role in improving living conditions and reducing the health risks associated with extreme heat. Fans help to prevent heatstroke and other heat-related illnesses by providing effective cooling and ventilation. In workplaces and industrial settings, electric fans have improved productivity and safety by maintaining comfortable temperatures and reducing the risk of overheating.

The development and widespread adoption of air conditioning in the mid-20th century did not diminish the importance of electric fans. In fact, fans and air conditioning systems often work in tandem to provide optimal cooling and energy efficiency. Fans help to circulate cool air generated by air conditioning units, allowing for more even distribution and reducing the overall energy consumption required to maintain comfortable temperatures. Additionally, fans are often used in situations where air conditioning is impractical or too costly, providing a more affordable and environmentally friendly cooling solution.

The electric fan has also found applications beyond cooling and ventilation. In agriculture, fans are used to provide airflow in greenhouses and livestock facilities, promoting healthy plant growth and animal welfare. In industrial processes, fans are used for drying, cooling machinery, and ventilating workspaces. The versatility and reliability of electric fans have made them indispensable tools in a wide range of settings.

In recent years, the focus on energy efficiency and sustainability has driven further innovation in electric fan technology. Manufacturers are developing fans with energy-efficient motors, improved blade designs, and advanced control systems to reduce power consumption and environmental impact. The integration of smart technology has also enhanced the functionality and convenience of electric fans. Smart fans can be controlled remotely via smartphones or voice assistants, allowing users to adjust settings and monitor energy usage with ease.

Chapter 21: The Path of the Sunglasses

The path of sunglasses from rudimentary sunshields to fashion staples and essential eye protection devices spans centuries, involving numerous cultural, technological, and scientific advancements. Sunglasses, now an indispensable accessory, have a rich history that reflects human ingenuity and the quest for comfort and style in the face of harsh sunlight.

The earliest known attempts to protect the eyes from the sun's glare date back to prehistoric times. Inuit peoples used flattened walrus ivory with narrow slits to protect their eyes from the harsh Arctic sunlight reflecting off snow and ice. These primitive goggles, known as "snow goggles," were essential for preventing snow blindness, a painful condition caused by overexposure to ultraviolet (UV) rays. The slits in the ivory reduced the amount of light entering the eyes while allowing the wearer to see adequately.

In ancient China, around the 12th century, judges used flat panes of smoky quartz to protect their eyes from the sun and to hide their expressions while interrogating witnesses. These early sunglasses were not designed to improve vision but to serve a functional and psychological purpose. The smoky quartz reduced glare, and the dark lenses masked the judges' eyes, adding an element of mystery and intimidation to the judicial process.

The use of tinted lenses spread to Europe in the 18th century, where they were primarily used for therapeutic purposes. The "Claude Lorraine" glasses, named after the French painter Claude Lorrain, featured lightly tinted lenses and were used by people suffering from syphilis, which caused sensitivity to light. These early sunglasses were rudimentary and lacked the ability to block harmful UV rays, but they marked the beginning of the use of tinted lenses for eye protection.

The 19th century saw significant advancements in the development of sunglasses. James Ayscough, an English optician, experimented with tinted lenses in the mid-1700s, believing that blue or green-tinted glass could correct specific vision problems. Although his ideas about color correction were not accurate, Ayscough's experiments contributed to the broader acceptance and use of tinted lenses.

The true evolution of modern sunglasses began in the early 20th century with the advent of affordable and effective UV protection. In 1929, Sam Foster, the founder of Foster Grant, began mass-producing sunglasses and selling them on the beaches of Atlantic City, New Jersey. Foster's sunglasses were designed to protect the eyes from the sun's harmful rays and quickly gained popularity among beachgoers. This marked the beginning of sunglasses as a consumer product widely accessible to the public.

During the 1930s, sunglasses gained further popularity due to their association with Hollywood and celebrity culture. Movie stars were frequently photographed wearing sunglasses, both on and off the set, which helped to establish them as a fashionable accessory. Sunglasses became synonymous with glamour, mystery, and sophistication, appealing to the public's desire to emulate their favorite stars.

In addition to their fashion appeal, sunglasses also became recognized for their practical benefits. The U.S. Army Air Corps, the precursor to the Air Force, commissioned Bausch & Lomb to develop sunglasses that would reduce pilots' glare and improve visibility during flight. In 1936, Bausch & Lomb introduced the iconic Aviator sunglasses, featuring green-tinted lenses designed to reduce glare without distorting colors. The Aviator style quickly became popular among military personnel and civilians alike, cementing its status as a timeless classic.

World War II further accelerated the adoption of sunglasses as essential eye protection. Pilots, soldiers, and sailors relied on sunglasses to protect their eyes from intense sunlight and glare, whether flying at high altitudes, navigating the seas, or operating in desert environments.

The functionality and practicality of sunglasses were proven in these extreme conditions, reinforcing their value as a protective accessory.

The post-war era saw an explosion in the popularity of sunglasses, driven by advancements in lens technology, materials, and manufacturing processes. In the 1960s, polarized lenses were introduced, providing superior glare reduction and visual clarity. Invented by Edwin H. Land, the founder of Polaroid Corporation, polarized lenses contain a special filter that blocks horizontally polarized light, which is the primary cause of glare from surfaces like water, snow, and roads. This innovation significantly enhanced the performance of sunglasses for outdoor activities such as driving, fishing, and skiing.

The 1970s and 1980s witnessed a surge in the popularity of sunglasses as a fashion statement. Designer brands such as Ray-Ban, Oakley, and Persol began to dominate the market, offering a wide range of styles and designs to suit different tastes and preferences. Ray-Ban's Wayfarer model, introduced in 1956, became an iconic symbol of rebellious cool, popularized by celebrities such as James Dean and Audrey Hepburn. The Wayfarer's bold, distinctive design and association with pop culture icons contributed to its enduring appeal.

The 1980s also saw the rise of Oakley, a brand known for its high-performance sunglasses designed for athletes and outdoor enthusiasts. Oakley's innovative designs and cutting-edge technology, including impact-resistant lenses and ergonomic frames, set a new standard for sport-specific eyewear. The brand's popularity grew rapidly, particularly among cyclists, skiers, and surfers, who valued the combination of style and functionality.

Throughout the late 20th century and into the 21st century, sunglasses continued to evolve, incorporating new technologies and materials to enhance their performance and durability. Advances in lens technology, such as the development of photochromic lenses that automatically adjust their tint based on light conditions, provided users with greater convenience and versatility. Additionally, improvements in UV protection ensured that modern sunglasses offered comprehensive protection against the sun's harmful rays.

The growing awareness of the dangers of UV radiation and its impact on eye health further drove the adoption of sunglasses. Prolonged exposure to UV rays can lead to various eye conditions, including cataracts, macular degeneration, and photokeratitis (sunburn of the cornea). Health organizations and eye care professionals increasingly emphasized the importance of wearing sunglasses with proper UV protection, leading to a greater emphasis on the functional benefits of sunglasses in addition to their aesthetic appeal.

The fashion industry has also played a significant role in shaping the evolution of sunglasses. Designers and fashion houses regularly release new collections and collaborate with celebrities and influencers to create limited-edition and signature styles. This constant innovation and trend-setting have ensured that sunglasses remain a dynamic and essential accessory in the world of fashion. Sunglasses have transcended their utilitarian origins to become a symbol of personal style and self-expression.

In recent years, sustainability has become a key focus in the production of sunglasses. As environmental concerns have grown, manufacturers have sought to reduce their carbon footprint and minimize the environmental impact of their products. This has led to the development of eco-friendly sunglasses made from recycled materials, biodegradable plastics, and sustainably sourced wood. Brands like Parafina and Pela have pioneered the use of sustainable materials in their eyewear collections, appealing to environmentally conscious consumers.

The digital age has also influenced the design and functionality of sunglasses. The proliferation of digital screens in our daily lives has increased the need for protection against blue light, which can cause eye strain and disrupt sleep patterns. In response, manufacturers have developed sunglasses with blue light filtering lenses, offering protection from both UV rays and digital eye strain. Additionally, smart sunglasses equipped with technology such as Bluetooth connectivity, integrated headphones, and augmented reality displays have emerged, blending style with cutting-edge functionality.

The path of sunglasses from primitive sunshields to high-tech fashion accessories reflects the continuous interplay between innovation, fashion, and functionality. Each stage of their evolution has been marked by significant advancements in materials, technology, and design, driven by the changing needs and desires of consumers.

Chapter 22: The Birth of the Plastic Bottle

The birth of the plastic bottle is a story intertwined with the rise of modern chemistry, industrial innovation, consumer culture, and environmental concerns. The plastic bottle, a ubiquitous object in contemporary life, traces its origins back to significant scientific discoveries and technological advancements over the past century. Its journey from a laboratory curiosity to a global staple highlights the complex interplay between convenience, consumer demand, and sustainability.

The story begins in the 19th century with the advent of synthetic polymers, which laid the groundwork for the development of plastics. The first synthetic polymer, Bakelite, was created by Belgian chemist Leo Baekeland in 1907. Bakelite was primarily used for electrical insulators and consumer goods, but it marked the beginning of the plastics industry. However, Bakelite was not suitable for making bottles due to its rigidity and brittleness.

The breakthrough for flexible and durable plastics came with the development of polyethylene in the 1930s and 1940s. British chemists Eric Fawcett and Reginald Gibson accidentally discovered polyethylene in 1933 while experimenting with high-pressure chemical reactions. Their work was further refined by American chemists at DuPont, leading to the commercialization of low-density polyethylene (LDPE) in 1941. LDPE was flexible, durable, and could be molded into various shapes, making it an ideal material for packaging.

Despite these advancements, glass remained the dominant material for bottles through the mid-20th century. Glass bottles were favored for their durability, impermeability, and inertness, making them suitable for storing a wide range of liquids. However, glass bottles were heavy, fragile, and expensive to produce and transport. These limitations drove the search for alternative materials that could offer the same benefits without the drawbacks.

The next significant milestone in the development of plastic bottles came in the 1950s with the invention of high-density polyethylene (HDPE). HDPE, developed by Karl Ziegler and Erhard Holzkamp in Germany, was stronger and more rigid than LDPE, making it suitable for blow molding into bottles. Blow molding is a manufacturing process that involves inflating a heated plastic tube within a mold to form a hollow container. This process allowed for the mass production of lightweight, durable, and inexpensive plastic bottles.

The commercialization of HDPE bottles began in the late 1950s and early 1960s, initially for non-food products such as detergents and shampoos. These early plastic bottles were praised for their unbreakable nature, light weight, and ease of production. However, concerns about the safety of using plastics for food and beverages delayed their widespread adoption in the food industry.

The real game-changer for plastic bottles came with the development of polyethylene terephthalate (PET) in the 1970s. PET was first synthesized in the 1940s by British chemists John Rex Whinfield and James Tennant Dickson, but its potential for use in packaging was not fully realized until decades later. PET is a thermoplastic polymer that is lightweight, strong, and highly resistant to impact and chemical degradation. It also has excellent barrier properties, making it ideal for containing carbonated beverages and other liquids.

In 1973, chemist Nathaniel Wyeth, working for DuPont, patented the PET bottle. Wyeth's design addressed the challenges of containing pressurized liquids like carbonated sodas, which required a material that could withstand internal pressure without deforming or leaking. The PET bottle quickly gained popularity in the beverage industry, revolutionizing the market for soft drinks and bottled water. PET bottles were not only lighter and more durable than glass bottles, but they were also cheaper to produce and transport, leading to significant cost savings for manufacturers and consumers.

The 1980s and 1990s saw an explosion in the use of PET bottles across various industries. The versatility of PET allowed it to be used for a wide range of products, including juices, cooking oils, salad dressings, and pharmaceuticals. The ability to create clear, transparent bottles that showcased the product inside further enhanced the appeal of PET bottles to both manufacturers and consumers. Additionally, advances in recycling technology made PET bottles more environmentally friendly, as they could be collected, processed, and repurposed into new bottles or other products.

The convenience and affordability of plastic bottles led to a rapid increase in their production and consumption. By the early 21st century, plastic bottles had become ubiquitous in daily life, with billions of bottles being produced and used each year worldwide. The global bottled water market, in particular, experienced exponential growth, driven by consumer demand for safe, portable, and convenient hydration options.

However, the widespread use of plastic bottles also brought significant environmental challenges. The durability that made plastic bottles so appealing also meant that they did not degrade easily in the environment. Plastic waste, including discarded bottles, began to accumulate in landfills, oceans, and natural landscapes, leading to severe ecological consequences. Marine life, in particular, suffered from the ingestion of plastic debris, which could cause injury or death. The issue of plastic pollution became a pressing global concern, prompting calls for more sustainable packaging solutions and waste management practices.

In response to these challenges, efforts to improve the sustainability of plastic bottles have intensified in recent years. Innovations in biodegradable plastics, such as polylactic acid (PLA) and polyhydroxyalkanoates (PHA), offer potential alternatives to traditional PET and HDPE bottles. These biodegradable plastics are designed to break down more quickly in the environment, reducing the long-term impact of plastic waste. However, they currently face challenges related to cost, performance, and large-scale production.

Recycling remains a key strategy for mitigating the environmental impact of plastic bottles. Many countries have implemented recycling programs and deposit return schemes to encourage the collection and recycling of plastic bottles. Advances in recycling technology have improved the efficiency and quality of recycled PET (rPET), enabling its use in the production of new bottles and other products. The use of rPET reduces the demand for virgin plastic and lowers the overall carbon footprint of plastic bottle production.

The development of closed-loop recycling systems, where plastic bottles are continuously recycled into new bottles, represents an important step towards a more sustainable future. Companies like Coca-Cola and PepsiCo have committed to increasing the use of rPET in their packaging and achieving higher recycling rates. These initiatives, combined with consumer education and regulatory support, aim to create a more circular economy for plastic bottles.

The emergence of reusable bottles has also gained traction as an alternative to single-use plastic bottles. Brands like Nalgene, S'well, and Hydro Flask have popularized durable, reusable bottles made from materials such as stainless steel, glass, and BPA-free plastic. These bottles are designed for long-term use and can significantly reduce the consumption of single-use plastic bottles. Public awareness campaigns and policies promoting the use of refillable bottles have contributed to this shift towards more sustainable hydration solutions.

Technological innovations continue to shape the future of plastic bottles. Smart packaging technologies, such as RFID tags and QR codes, are being integrated into plastic bottles to improve traceability, enhance recycling, and provide consumers with information about the product and its environmental impact. These advancements have the potential to create more transparent and efficient supply chains, ultimately contributing to better resource management and waste reduction.

The journey of the plastic bottle from a laboratory experiment to a global phenomenon reflects the complex interplay between scientific discovery, industrial innovation, consumer behavior, and environmental stewardship. While plastic bottles have brought significant convenience and economic benefits, they have also posed serious environmental challenges that require collective action and innovation to address.

Chapter 23: The Transformation of the Shopping Cart

The transformation of the shopping cart is a fascinating journey that illustrates the evolution of retail practices, consumer behavior, and technological advancements over the past century. From its humble beginnings as a simple wireframe structure to the sophisticated, tech-enabled carts of today, the shopping cart has undergone significant changes that reflect broader trends in commerce and society.

The story of the shopping cart begins in the 1930s with the rise of the supermarket. Before the advent of supermarkets, most consumers shopped at small, specialized stores such as bakeries, butcher shops, and greengrocers. Shoppers would hand their lists to clerks who would then fetch the items, a process that was both time-consuming and labor-intensive. The concept of the self-service store emerged in the early 20th century, revolutionizing the shopping experience by allowing customers to select their own goods. However, as shoppers began to purchase more items, carrying baskets quickly became cumbersome.

In 1937, Sylvan Goldman, owner of the Humpty Dumpty supermarket chain in Oklahoma, invented the first shopping cart. Goldman's innovation was inspired by observing customers struggling with heavy baskets. He envisioned a wheeled device that would enable shoppers to carry more items with less effort. With the help of mechanic Fred Young, Goldman developed a folding, wheeled cart that could hold two wire baskets. The initial design featured a metal frame with four wheels, a handle for pushing, and a foldable mechanism for easy storage. Goldman introduced the carts in his stores, marketing them as a convenient solution for shoppers.

Despite the practicality of Goldman's invention, the early reception was lukewarm. Many customers were hesitant to use the carts, fearing they would look lazy or that the carts were too cumbersome. To overcome this resistance, Goldman hired actors to push the carts around his stores, demonstrating their convenience and ease of use. This clever marketing strategy eventually paid off, and the shopping cart began to gain acceptance. By the early 1940s, shopping carts had become a common feature in supermarkets across the United States.

The next major evolution in shopping cart design came in the 1940s and 1950s, driven by the need for greater durability and capacity. The original folding carts were prone to wear and tear, and their limited capacity could not keep up with the growing demand for larger grocery hauls. In response, designers began to experiment with sturdier materials and more robust construction methods. The introduction of larger, one-piece wire baskets improved the durability and usability of shopping carts. These new designs could carry more items and withstand the rigors of daily use.

The 1960s and 1970s saw further refinements in shopping cart design, as well as the emergence of additional features to enhance the shopping experience. One notable innovation was the child seat, introduced in the early 1960s. The child seat allowed parents to safely secure their children in the cart while shopping, making it easier and more convenient for families to shop together. The inclusion of a fold-out seat also provided a practical solution for accommodating young children without compromising the cart's storage capacity.

During this period, shopping cart manufacturers also began to explore the use of different materials to improve the carts' performance and longevity. The introduction of plastic-coated wire baskets and plastic components helped to reduce noise, prevent rust, and extend the lifespan of the carts. These advancements contributed to the widespread adoption of shopping carts in supermarkets and other retail environments.

The 1980s and 1990s marked a period of significant innovation and diversification in shopping cart design. The rise of big-box stores and warehouse clubs, such as Walmart and Costco, created demand for even larger and more robust carts. These stores sold items in bulk, requiring carts with greater capacity and sturdiness. In response, manufacturers developed oversized carts with reinforced frames and larger wheels to accommodate heavier loads. The introduction of nesting carts, which could be pushed together and stored compactly, addressed the need for efficient storage in large retail spaces.

In addition to larger carts, the 1980s and 1990s saw the emergence of specialized carts tailored to specific retail environments. For example, home improvement stores like Home Depot and Lowe's introduced flatbed carts and lumber carts designed to transport large, bulky items such as plywood and construction materials. These specialized carts featured flat, open platforms with minimal sides, allowing for easy loading and unloading of oversized goods. Garden centers and nurseries also adopted unique cart designs, such as wire mesh garden carts with high sides and larger wheels for maneuvering over rough terrain.

The turn of the 21st century brought new technological advancements that began to transform the humble shopping cart into a more sophisticated tool. The introduction of barcode scanning and radio-frequency identification (RFID) technology allowed retailers to track inventory and monitor the movement of shopping carts within the store. Smart shopping carts equipped with digital displays and sensors offered customers a more interactive shopping experience, providing product information, promotions, and personalized recommendations based on their shopping history.

One of the most significant technological innovations in recent years has been the development of autonomous shopping carts. These carts are equipped with sensors, cameras, and artificial intelligence (AI) systems that enable them to navigate the store independently, following customers and carrying their items. Autonomous carts are designed to reduce the physical strain of pushing a heavy cart and enhance the overall shopping experience. Companies like Walmart and Amazon have been at the forefront of testing and implementing these autonomous systems in their stores.

The integration of mobile technology has further enhanced the functionality of shopping carts. Many retailers now offer mobile apps that allow customers to create shopping lists, locate items within the store, and even pay for their purchases directly from their smartphones. Some smart carts are equipped with tablet-like interfaces that sync with these mobile apps, providing real-time updates and personalized assistance as customers shop. These innovations aim to streamline the shopping process, reduce wait times, and improve customer satisfaction.

Environmental concerns and sustainability have also played a significant role in the ongoing transformation of shopping carts. The increasing awareness of plastic pollution and the push for eco-friendly practices have led to the development of shopping carts made from recycled and sustainable materials. Some manufacturers have introduced carts made from recycled plastics, aluminum, and even bamboo, reducing the environmental impact of cart production and disposal. Additionally, the rise of reusable shopping bags has prompted some retailers to design carts with dedicated hooks or compartments for holding these bags, encouraging customers to adopt more sustainable shopping habits.

The COVID-19 pandemic brought new challenges and changes to the shopping cart's evolution. As concerns about hygiene and safety became paramount, retailers implemented measures to sanitize carts more frequently and introduced touchless technologies to minimize physical contact. Innovations such as UV-C light sanitation systems and antimicrobial coatings on cart handles were developed to enhance the safety and cleanliness of shopping carts. These measures addressed immediate health concerns and set new standards for hygiene in retail environments.

The transformation of the shopping cart reflects broader trends in retail and consumer behavior. As shopping habits continue to evolve, so too will the design and functionality of shopping carts. The rise of e-commerce and online grocery shopping has led some retailers to explore hybrid models that integrate traditional in-store shopping with digital conveniences. For example, some stores now offer "click and collect" services, where customers can place orders online and pick up their items in-store using specially designated shopping carts.

Looking ahead, the future of shopping carts will likely be shaped by ongoing advancements in technology, sustainability, and consumer preferences. The integration of AI, machine learning, and data analytics will enable even smarter and more personalized shopping experiences. As retailers seek to enhance customer engagement and streamline operations, shopping carts will continue to play a crucial role in the evolving landscape of retail.

The journey of the shopping cart, from its inception in the 1930s to its current status as a multifunctional tool, highlights the dynamic nature of retail innovation. The shopping cart's evolution reflects the changing needs and expectations of consumers, as well as the continuous pursuit of convenience, efficiency, and sustainability in the retail industry. As we move forward, the shopping cart will undoubtedly continue to adapt and transform, remaining an essential component of the shopping experience for generations to come.

Chapter 24: The Journey of the Postcard

The journey of the postcard is a fascinating exploration of cultural, technological, and social evolution spanning more than a century. From its humble beginnings as a simple means of communication to its status as a cherished memento of travel and personal connection, the postcard has witnessed and adapted to significant changes in society and technology. The story of the postcard is not just about a piece of printed cardboard; it's about how people communicate, share experiences, and preserve memories across time and distance.

The concept of the postcard can be traced back to the mid-19th century. Before postcards, communication was primarily conducted through letters, which required envelopes and often lengthy compositions. The idea of a simpler, more efficient way to send short messages began to take shape in various countries. In 1865, Dr. Heinrich von Stephan, a Prussian postal official, proposed the idea of a "postblatt," or open post sheet, at a postal conference. Although his idea was initially rejected, it set the stage for future developments.

The first official postcards were introduced in Austria-Hungary in 1869 by Dr. Emanuel Herrmann. Recognizing the need for a more convenient and cost-effective means of communication, Herrmann advocated for the creation of a card that could be sent without an envelope. On October 1, 1869, the Austrian government issued the world's first postcard, known as the "Correspondenz-Karte." This card featured a pre-printed stamp and space for a brief message, allowing for quick and easy communication. The concept quickly gained popularity, and other countries soon followed suit.

In the United States, postcards were officially introduced in 1873 by the Post Office Department. The first American postcards, known as "postal cards," were plain, government-issued cards that featured pre-printed postage and space for a short message. These early postcards were primarily used for business correspondence and short notes. Private companies were not yet permitted to print postcards, which limited their design and usage.

The next major development in the postcard's journey came in the 1890s with the advent of the "divided back" postcard. Before this innovation, postcards had a blank back, with one side reserved for the address and the other for the message. The divided back, which allowed for a message on one side and the address on the other, revolutionized postcard design and usage. This change coincided with the rise of tourism and travel, as well as advancements in printing technology that made it easier to produce colorful and attractive postcards.

The "Golden Age" of postcards, roughly from 1900 to 1915, marked a period of explosive growth and popularity. During this time, postcards became a ubiquitous form of communication and a popular collectible. Advances in printing techniques, such as chromolithography, allowed for the production of high-quality, vibrant postcards featuring scenic views, landmarks, humorous illustrations, and artistic designs. Postcards became souvenirs of travel, tokens of affection, and means of sharing experiences with friends and family. The popularity of postcards was further fueled by the establishment of the Universal Postal Union in 1874, which standardized international postal rates and facilitated the global exchange of mail.

The early 20th century also saw the rise of real photo postcards (RPPCs), which were photographic images printed directly onto postcard stock. RPPCs provided a unique and personal way to capture and share moments, as they often featured portraits, local scenes, and significant events. These postcards were particularly popular in rural areas, where professional photographers would travel from town to town, offering their services to create custom postcards for residents.

World War I had a significant impact on the postcard industry. During the war, postcards were used extensively by soldiers and civilians to stay in touch with loved ones. Military-themed postcards, featuring patriotic imagery, portraits of soldiers, and scenes from the front lines, became widespread. These postcards served as a crucial means of communication and morale-boosting during a time of separation and uncertainty.

The interwar period and the advent of the "linen era" in the 1930s brought further changes to postcard production. Linen postcards were printed on textured paper with a high rag content, giving them a distinctive look and feel. The use of vibrant colors and bold designs made linen postcards particularly popular for depicting travel destinations, national parks, and cityscapes. This era also saw the rise of large letter postcards, which featured the names of cities or states in oversized, colorful letters filled with images of local attractions.

The post-World War II era marked the beginning of the "chrome era," characterized by the use of glossy, color-rich printing techniques. Chrome postcards, named for their glossy finish, became the standard for postcards from the 1950s onward. Advances in photography and printing technology allowed for the production of highly detailed, full-color images that captured the beauty of travel destinations, landmarks, and everyday life. The chrome era coincided with the postwar economic boom and the rise of mass tourism, further cementing the postcard's role as a travel souvenir and means of communication.

The late 20th century brought new challenges and changes to the postcard industry. The advent of digital communication, including email and social media, began to overshadow traditional mail. Despite this shift, postcards continued to hold a special place in the hearts of many as tangible mementos of travel and personal connections. Collectors, known as deltiologists, continued to cherish vintage postcards for their historical and artistic value, preserving them as artifacts of cultural and social history.

In recent years, the postcard has experienced a resurgence in popularity, driven by a renewed appreciation for analog communication and the unique qualities of physical mail. The rise of postcard exchange networks, such as Postcrossing, has brought together postcard enthusiasts from around the world, encouraging the exchange of postcards across borders and fostering a global community of collectors and correspondents. Social media platforms have also played a role in revitalizing interest in postcards, as users share images of their collections and connect with fellow enthusiasts.

The postcard's journey is also marked by its role as a medium for artistic expression and social commentary. Throughout its history, postcards have been used by artists, photographers, and designers to showcase their work and convey messages. From the Art Nouveau and Art Deco movements to contemporary graphic design, postcards have served as a canvas for creative expression. They have also been used for political and social activism, with postcards featuring slogans, images, and messages advocating for various causes and movements.

Environmental concerns and sustainability have become increasingly important in recent years, prompting discussions about the impact of postcards on the environment. While postcards are made from paper, a renewable resource, the production and transportation of postcards contribute to carbon emissions and deforestation. In response, some companies and organizations have begun to explore more sustainable practices, such as using recycled paper, eco-friendly inks, and carbon offset programs to reduce the environmental footprint of postcards.

The future of the postcard is likely to be shaped by ongoing technological advancements and evolving consumer preferences. Augmented reality (AR) and other digital technologies have the potential to enhance the postcard experience, allowing recipients to view interactive content or personalized messages through their smartphones. Hybrid postcards, which combine physical and digital elements, may become more common, offering a unique blend of tradition and innovation.

Despite the challenges posed by digital communication, the postcard's enduring appeal lies in its tangible, personal nature. Unlike an email or text message, a postcard is a physical object that can be held, displayed, and cherished. The act of selecting a postcard, writing a message, and sending it through the mail carries a sense of intention and thoughtfulness that digital communication often lacks. For many, receiving a postcard is a small but meaningful gesture that brightens their day and strengthens their connection with the sender.

The postcard's journey from a simple means of communication to a beloved cultural artifact reflects the broader trends and changes in society over the past century. As a symbol of travel, personal connection, and artistic expression, the postcard continues to hold a special place in our hearts and lives. Its story is a testament to the enduring power of human connection and the ways in which we adapt and innovate to stay connected across time and distance.

Chapter 25: The Invention of the Paper Towel

The invention of the paper towel is a story that reflects innovation, practical problem-solving, and the impact of industrial advances on everyday life. Paper towels, now a ubiquitous household item, were born out of necessity and have since become an indispensable part of modern living, serving a variety of functions from cleaning to personal hygiene. Their journey from conception to widespread use is a fascinating tale that involves creativity, perseverance, and a deep understanding of consumer needs.

The origins of the paper towel can be traced back to the early 20th century. The story begins with a serendipitous mistake at the Scott Paper Company, a leading manufacturer of toilet paper. In 1907, the company produced a batch of toilet paper that was too thick to be used for its intended purpose. Rather than discarding the unusable product, Arthur Scott, the company's founder, saw an opportunity to repurpose it. He decided to cut the thick paper into small, individual sheets and market them as disposable hand towels. This marked the birth of the paper towel as a distinct product.

Arthur Scott's initial idea was to address a specific need in public restrooms. At the time, cloth towels were commonly used in public facilities, but they posed significant hygiene risks. Cloth towels could harbor bacteria and spread germs, particularly in high-traffic areas. Scott recognized that disposable paper towels could provide a more sanitary alternative. The first paper towels were marketed under the name "Sani-Towels," emphasizing their hygienic benefits. These early paper towels were designed to be used once and then discarded, reducing the risk of contamination and promoting better public health.

The introduction of Sani-Towels was a modest success, but it laid the groundwork for the development of a more versatile product. The concept of a disposable paper towel resonated with consumers, and Scott continued to refine and improve the design. By the 1920s, paper towels were being marketed for use in kitchens and households, not just public restrooms. The product's convenience and effectiveness quickly gained popularity, leading to increased demand and further innovation.

One of the key milestones in the evolution of paper towels was the development of the "kitchen towel" in the 1930s. This new iteration of the paper towel was specifically designed for household use, offering a convenient solution for cleaning up spills, wiping surfaces, and performing a variety of other tasks. The kitchen towel was made from a more absorbent and durable paper, allowing it to handle tougher cleaning jobs. The Scott Paper Company played a pivotal role in popularizing this new product, emphasizing its versatility and practicality in their marketing campaigns.

The widespread adoption of paper towels in households was driven by several factors. First and foremost, the convenience of disposable paper towels resonated with consumers who were looking for ways to simplify their daily chores. Unlike cloth towels, which needed to be washed and dried after each use, paper towels could be used once and then discarded, saving time and effort. This convenience was particularly appealing in the context of the rapid pace of modern life, where efficiency and ease of use were highly valued.

Another important factor was the growing awareness of hygiene and cleanliness in the early 20th century. As scientific understanding of germs and bacteria advanced, there was a greater emphasis on maintaining sanitary conditions in both public and private spaces. Paper towels, with their disposable nature, offered a hygienic alternative to reusable cloth towels, which could become breeding grounds for germs if not properly washed. This health-conscious mindset contributed to the increasing popularity of paper towels as a household staple.

The production and distribution of paper towels also benefited from advances in industrial manufacturing and transportation. The development of new papermaking technologies and machinery allowed for the mass production of paper towels at a lower cost, making them more affordable for consumers. Improvements in transportation infrastructure facilitated the distribution of paper towels to a wider market, expanding their availability beyond urban centers to rural and suburban areas. These advancements helped to establish paper towels as a common household item across the United States.

In the decades following the introduction of kitchen towels, paper towel manufacturers continued to innovate and improve their products. One notable innovation was the development of two-ply paper towels in the 1960s. Two-ply paper towels consisted of two layers of paper bonded together, providing increased strength and absorbency. This advancement allowed paper towels to handle larger spills and tougher cleaning tasks more effectively. The introduction of perforated rolls also made it easier for consumers to tear off individual sheets, adding to the convenience and functionality of paper towels.

The marketing strategies employed by paper towel manufacturers played a crucial role in shaping consumer perceptions and driving demand. Companies like Scott Paper, Bounty, and Brawny invested heavily in advertising campaigns that highlighted the superior absorbency, strength, and versatility of their products. Catchy slogans, memorable jingles, and television commercials featuring demonstrations of paper towels' effectiveness helped to establish brand recognition and loyalty. These marketing efforts emphasized the practical benefits of paper towels, positioning them as an essential tool for modern households.

The environmental impact of paper towels has been a topic of concern and debate in recent years. The production of paper towels requires significant amounts of water, energy, and raw materials, contributing to deforestation and pollution. Additionally, the disposable nature of paper towels generates large quantities of waste, putting pressure on landfills and waste management systems. In response to these concerns, manufacturers have explored more sustainable practices, such as using recycled materials, reducing packaging, and improving production efficiency.

The rise of eco-friendly alternatives has also influenced the paper towel market. Reusable cloth towels, biodegradable paper towels, and bamboo-based products have gained popularity among environmentally conscious consumers. These alternatives offer a more sustainable option for those looking to reduce their environmental footprint while still enjoying the convenience of disposable paper towels. The shift towards sustainability reflects a broader trend in consumer behavior, where environmental considerations are increasingly factored into purchasing decisions.

Despite the challenges posed by environmental concerns, paper towels remain a popular and widely used product. Their versatility and convenience continue to make them an indispensable part of everyday life. In addition to their traditional uses in kitchens and bathrooms, paper towels have found applications in a variety of settings, including offices, schools, hospitals, and industrial facilities. They are used for everything from cleaning and sanitizing surfaces to drying hands and wiping up spills.

The COVID-19 pandemic underscored the importance of paper towels in maintaining hygiene and cleanliness. As concerns about virus transmission and sanitation grew, the demand for paper towels surged. Consumers stocked up on paper towels as part of their efforts to keep their homes and workplaces clean and safe. Manufacturers ramped up production to meet the increased demand, highlighting the critical role that paper towels play in public health and hygiene.

The future of paper towels will likely be shaped by ongoing technological advancements and changing consumer preferences. Innovations in materials science and manufacturing processes have the potential to improve the performance and sustainability of paper towels. For example, research into biodegradable and compostable materials could lead to the development of paper towels that break down more easily in the environment. Advances in nanotechnology and coatings could enhance the absorbency and durability of paper towels, making them even more effective for a wide range of tasks.

Consumer behavior and preferences will also continue to influence the paper towel market. The growing awareness of environmental issues is likely to drive demand for more sustainable products, prompting manufacturers to adopt greener practices and develop eco-friendly alternatives. At the same time, the convenience and effectiveness of traditional paper towels will ensure their continued popularity among consumers who prioritize practicality and ease of use.

Chapter 26: The Story of the Corkscrew

The story of the corkscrew is an intriguing journey through the history of innovation and human ingenuity. The corkscrew, a tool we often take for granted today, has a rich past rooted in the evolution of wine consumption and the need for practical solutions to everyday problems. It is a fascinating example of how a simple object can evolve over centuries to meet the changing demands of society.

The origins of the corkscrew can be traced back to the early 17th century. Prior to the invention of the corkscrew, wine bottles were sealed with wooden stoppers wrapped in oil-soaked rags or wax. These seals were difficult to remove, and as cork became the preferred method for sealing bottles, a new tool was needed to extract the corks effectively. The earliest known reference to a corkscrew-like device appears in a 1681 publication, where it was described as a "steel worm" used for drawing corks from bottles. This steel worm was inspired by a similar tool used by musketmen to remove unspent charges from their guns. The early corkscrews were rudimentary and resembled the gun worms used by soldiers, consisting of a simple metal spiral attached to a handle.

As wine consumption grew in popularity throughout Europe, particularly in France and England, the need for a more efficient and user-friendly corkscrew became apparent. By the 18th century, inventors began to focus on improving the design. In 1795, the first patent for a corkscrew was granted to the Reverend Samuel Henshall in England. Henshall's design featured a disk, later known as the Henshall Button, between the handle and the worm. This disk helped to prevent the worm from penetrating too deeply into the cork and provided leverage to extract it more easily. This innovation marked a significant improvement and set the stage for further refinements.

Throughout the 19th century, numerous inventors continued to refine the corkscrew, leading to a variety of designs and mechanisms.

In 1802, Edward Thomason of Birmingham, England, patented a corkscrew that incorporated a mechanical advantage through the use of a threaded shaft and a T-handle, making it easier to pull the cork from the bottle. This design became known as the Thomason Corkscrew and was widely popular for its efficiency. Other notable designs included the Rack and Pinion corkscrew, patented by John Ames in 1867, which used a gear mechanism to increase leverage, and the Lever corkscrew, patented by Carl Wienke in 1883, which employed a hinged lever to assist in removing the cork.

The late 19th and early 20th centuries saw the introduction of various innovative corkscrews that further simplified the process of opening wine bottles. In 1892, William Rockwell Clough patented a continuous helix corkscrew that allowed the user to pull the cork straight out without the need for back-and-forth twisting. This design, known as the Clough Corkscrew, became popular in the United States and was widely used in homes and restaurants. In 1920, the double-lever corkscrew, also known as the winged corkscrew or butterfly corkscrew, was patented by Dominick Rosati. This design featured two levers that were raised as the worm was twisted into the cork and then pushed down to extract the cork, making it easier for users with less strength.

The 20th century also saw the development of specialized corkscrews for different purposes. The Waiter's Friend, a pocket-sized corkscrew with a small knife for cutting foil, a worm, and a lever, became a favorite among waiters and sommeliers for its portability and functionality. The Ah-So corkscrew, which uses two prongs to slide down the sides of the cork and pull it out without piercing it, was invented to handle fragile or crumbling corks, preserving their integrity.

In recent decades, the corkscrew has continued to evolve with advancements in materials and technology. Modern corkscrews often feature ergonomic handles, non-stick coatings on the worm, and even electric or battery-operated mechanisms that make opening a bottle of wine virtually effortless. The Rabbit Corkscrew, introduced in the late 1990s, uses a lever and gear system to extract the cork in a single, smooth motion and has become a popular choice for wine enthusiasts.

The story of the corkscrew is not only about the evolution of a tool but also about the culture of wine and its significance in social and culinary traditions. Wine has been an integral part of human civilization for thousands of years, and the corkscrew has played a crucial role in making this beloved beverage more accessible and enjoyable. From the early days of struggling with wooden stoppers to the modern convenience of electric corkscrews, the history of the corkscrew reflects our ongoing quest for innovation and improvement in even the most everyday objects.

In addition to its functional evolution, the corkscrew has also become a collector's item and a symbol of craftsmanship. Antique corkscrews, particularly those from the 18th and 19th centuries, are highly sought after by collectors and can fetch high prices at auctions. These vintage corkscrews are often admired not only for their historical significance but also for their intricate designs and the skill required to produce them.

Chapter 27: The History of the Keychain

The history of the keychain is a remarkable journey that reflects the evolution of human society, technology, and design. The keychain, a small item that serves to keep keys together and accessible, has a surprisingly rich and varied history that spans centuries. Its development is intertwined with the invention of the key itself and the ways in which people have sought to secure their possessions and property.

Keys have existed for thousands of years, with the earliest known examples dating back to ancient Mesopotamia and Egypt around 4,000 years ago. These early keys were large and made of wood or metal, designed to operate similarly primitive locks. The concept of a keychain, however, did not emerge until much later, as keys themselves evolved to become smaller and more portable. The transition from bulky, single keys to the more compact, metal keys we recognize today began during the Roman Empire, where metalworking techniques allowed for the creation of more sophisticated and durable keys.

As keys became more common and essential for securing homes, chests, and other valuable items, the need to keep them organized and easily accessible grew. The earliest form of a keychain likely took the form of simple rings or loops of leather, string, or metal, used to bundle multiple keys together. These rudimentary keychains provided a practical solution to the problem of managing several keys and ensured that they could be carried conveniently. The development of the keychain paralleled the increasing complexity of locks and keys, driven by the need for better security and the proliferation of personal possessions requiring protection.

During the medieval period, keys continued to be important symbols of authority and security. They were often large, ornate, and worn on belts or carried in pouches by those in positions of power. Keychains, if they existed, were likely to be similarly ornate, crafted from precious metals and adorned with decorative elements to reflect the status of their owners. The Renaissance period saw further advancements in key and lock technology, with more intricate designs and mechanisms being developed. Keychains of this era, though still relatively simple, began to take on more personalized forms, incorporating unique designs and embellishments.

The industrial revolution in the 18th and 19th centuries brought significant changes to key and keychain manufacturing. Mass production techniques allowed for the creation of smaller, more standardized keys, making them more accessible to the general population. The keychain as a distinct object began to gain popularity, with a wider variety of materials and designs becoming available. Keychains were often made of metal and featured simple rings or hooks to hold keys. During this time, the functional aspect of the keychain was paramount, but decorative elements began to emerge as well.

The late 19th and early 20th centuries saw the rise of the modern keychain as we know it today. The advent of new materials such as plastic, along with advancements in metalworking and manufacturing, allowed for greater creativity and diversity in keychain design. Keychains began to be produced in a wide array of shapes, sizes, and styles, reflecting the tastes and interests of their owners. Souvenir keychains became popular, often featuring miniature landmarks, logos, or symbols representing different cities, countries, or events. These collectible keychains served as mementos of travel and experiences, adding a sentimental value to their practical function.

The 20th century also saw the keychain become a medium for advertising and promotion. Companies began to produce branded keychains as promotional items, distributing them to customers and clients as a way to keep their brand visible and top-of-mind. These promotional keychains were often simple in design, featuring the company's logo or name, but they played an important role in marketing strategies. The versatility and utility of keychains made them an ideal promotional tool, ensuring that the brand would be seen regularly as people used their keys in daily life.

In addition to their use as promotional items, keychains began to be seen as fashion accessories and expressions of personal style. The 1960s and 1970s, in particular, saw an explosion of creativity in keychain design, with a wide range of materials, colors, and themes being explored. Novelty keychains, featuring everything from miniature toys to humorous slogans, became popular, especially among young people. The keychain's ability to be customized and personalized made it a perfect canvas for self-expression.

The advent of digital technology in the late 20th and early 21st centuries brought new innovations to the keychain. Electronic key fobs, used to control car locks, garage doors, and even home security systems, became increasingly common. These key fobs often incorporated additional features such as panic buttons, remote start capabilities, and keyless entry systems. The integration of electronic components into keychains represented a significant shift, adding new layers of functionality and convenience.

In recent years, the keychain has continued to evolve with the advent of smart technology. Smart keychains, equipped with Bluetooth and GPS capabilities, can help users locate lost keys through their smartphones. These high-tech keychains often include additional features such as USB drives, LED lights, and bottle openers, further enhancing their utility. The design and production of keychains have also benefited from advancements in materials science, with durable and lightweight materials like aluminum, titanium, and high-grade plastics becoming more common.

Despite these technological advancements, the keychain has retained its fundamental purpose: to keep keys organized and accessible. Its enduring appeal lies in its simplicity and practicality, as well as its ability to serve as a canvas for creativity and personal expression. Keychains today come in an almost infinite variety of designs, from the simplest metal rings to intricate works of art, reflecting the diverse tastes and interests of people around the world.

Chapter 28: The Development of the Nail Clipper

The development of the nail clipper is a fascinating journey through human history, reflecting the evolution of personal grooming tools and the increasing sophistication of design and technology. The nail clipper, an essential item in modern personal care, has its roots in ancient times and has undergone significant transformations to become the efficient and ubiquitous tool we know today. This story intertwines advancements in metallurgy, industrialization, and changing cultural attitudes towards hygiene and grooming.

The concept of grooming tools for nails can be traced back to ancient civilizations. The earliest known implements for nail care were simple and rudimentary, often made from natural materials such as flint, bone, and later, metal. In ancient Egypt, for example, grooming was an important aspect of daily life, and both men and women used small metal tools to care for their nails. Similarly, in ancient Rome, nail care was an essential part of personal hygiene, and wealthy Romans often employed servants to maintain their nails using specialized tools made from iron and bronze.

During the Middle Ages, nail care continued to be practiced, although the tools remained relatively basic. Scissors and small knives were commonly used to trim nails, and these instruments required a certain level of skill and precision. As metallurgy advanced, more refined and durable tools became available, but the process of nail trimming was still largely manual and often cumbersome. It wasn't until the advent of the industrial revolution that significant changes began to occur in the design and production of nail care implements.

The industrial revolution, spanning from the late 18th to the early 19th century, brought about dramatic advancements in manufacturing and materials. Innovations in metallurgy and mass production techniques allowed for the creation of more precise and efficient tools. It was during this period that the precursor to the modern nail clipper began to take shape. Early versions of nail clippers were simple lever-action devices made from metal, designed to cut nails more effectively than scissors or knives. These early clippers were often handcrafted, reflecting the craftsmanship of the time.

One of the most significant milestones in the development of the nail clipper was the patenting of various designs in the 19th century. In 1875, Valentine Fogerty received a patent for a nail clipper that featured a lever and two cutting blades, a design that closely resembles modern clippers. Fogerty's invention was intended to make nail trimming easier and more efficient, reducing the risk of injury and providing a more uniform cut. This design was a significant improvement over previous methods and marked a turning point in the evolution of nail care tools.

As the 19th century progressed, further innovations and improvements were made to the nail clipper. In 1881, Eugene Heim and Celestin Matz received a patent for a new type of nail clipper that featured a pivoting lever and a concave cutting edge. This design allowed for a more precise and controlled cut, and its ergonomic shape made it easier to use. The Heim-Matz nail clipper became a popular choice and set the standard for subsequent designs.

The early 20th century saw the widespread adoption and commercialization of nail clippers. Advances in manufacturing techniques, particularly the use of stainless steel and other durable metals, allowed for the mass production of high-quality nail clippers at affordable prices. Companies such as the H. W. Carter & Sons Company and the Gem Manufacturing Company began producing nail clippers on a large scale, making them accessible to a broader audience. The increased availability of nail clippers coincided with changing cultural attitudes towards personal hygiene and grooming, further driving their popularity.

During this period, the design of nail clippers continued to be refined and optimized. The introduction of compound lever mechanisms, which provided greater cutting power with less effort, made nail clippers even more efficient and user-friendly. These compound lever clippers, often referred to as "double-lever" or "compound-action" clippers, featured two levers connected by a pivot, allowing for a smoother and more controlled cutting action. This design quickly became the standard and remains the most common type of nail clipper in use today.

In addition to the standard lever-action nail clippers, other designs and variations emerged to cater to different needs and preferences. For example, toenail clippers, which are typically larger and more robust than fingernail clippers, were developed to handle the thicker and tougher nails of the toes. Guillotine-style nail clippers, which use a single blade that cuts through the nail like a guillotine, became popular for their ease of use and precise cuts. Scissor-style nail clippers, which resemble small scissors with curved blades, offered an alternative for those who preferred a different cutting motion.

The mid-20th century saw further innovations in the materials and ergonomics of nail clippers. The introduction of plastic handles and grips provided greater comfort and control, reducing hand fatigue during use. Some nail clippers also incorporated additional features such as nail files, cuticle pushers, and nail cleaners, making them multi-functional grooming tools. These integrated designs appealed to consumers looking for convenience and versatility in their personal care products.

In recent decades, the design and functionality of nail clippers have continued to evolve, influenced by advancements in technology and changes in consumer preferences. Modern nail clippers often feature ergonomic designs with contoured handles and non-slip grips for enhanced comfort and control. Some high-end models are made from premium materials such as titanium or surgical-grade stainless steel, offering superior durability and precision. Innovations such as laser-cut blades and advanced hinge mechanisms have further improved the performance and longevity of nail clippers.

In addition to traditional manual nail clippers, electric and battery-operated models have also entered the market. These devices use motorized blades or rotating discs to trim nails quickly and effortlessly, catering to individuals with limited dexterity or strength. Some electric nail clippers also include built-in sensors to prevent over-cutting and ensure a safe and precise trim.

The development of the nail clipper is not only a story of technological innovation but also a reflection of changing social and cultural norms. As personal grooming became increasingly important in modern society, the demand for effective and convenient tools grew. Nail clippers, once a luxury item, became an essential part of daily hygiene routines for people of all ages and backgrounds. The widespread availability of affordable nail clippers democratized personal care, making it possible for everyone to maintain well-groomed nails.

Today, nail clippers are available in a wide variety of designs, sizes, and price points, catering to different needs and preferences. From basic, no-frills models to high-end, precision-engineered tools, there is a nail clipper for every user. The continued innovation in design and materials ensures that nail clippers remain an indispensable part of personal grooming routines around the world.

Chapter 29: The Evolution of the Measuring Tape

The evolution of the measuring tape is a story that spans centuries and reflects the profound advancements in technology, craftsmanship, and the human need for precision and accuracy in various fields. From the earliest rudimentary tools used to gauge distances to the modern, highly accurate devices used in construction, tailoring, and other industries, the measuring tape has undergone significant transformations that highlight human ingenuity and the quest for improvement.

The origins of the measuring tape can be traced back to ancient civilizations, where early humans used natural elements to measure distances. The Egyptians, for example, used a unit of measure called the cubit, based on the length of the forearm from the elbow to the tip of the middle finger. They employed ropes and strings with knots tied at regular intervals to create standardized lengths, which were crucial for building the pyramids and other architectural feats. Similarly, the Romans used a measurement called the pace (passus), which was the distance covered in a double step, and created measuring tools such as the Roman foot, made from metal or wood, to ensure uniformity in their constructions.

These early measuring devices, while innovative for their time, were limited by the materials available and the need for standardization. The Middle Ages saw the continued use of these basic measuring tools, but it wasn't until the Renaissance period, with its emphasis on science, mathematics, and precision, that significant advancements were made. The Renaissance brought about the creation of more accurate and standardized tools, driven by the needs of architects, engineers, and scientists. One notable invention was the folding rule, which appeared in the 16th century. These early folding rules were typically made of wood or ivory and featured joints that allowed the ruler to fold into a compact size, making it easier to carry.

The true precursor to the modern measuring tape emerged during the Industrial Revolution in the 18th and 19th centuries. This period marked a significant shift in manufacturing and materials science, leading to the development of more sophisticated and durable tools. In 1821, the first patented design for a flexible measuring device was created by the Englishman James Chesterman. Chesterman's invention consisted of a steel tape, which was flexible yet strong, coiled inside a leather case. This innovation allowed for a much longer measuring tape than was possible with rigid rulers or folding rules, and it could be easily retracted and carried. Chesterman's steel tape measure quickly gained popularity, particularly among surveyors and builders, due to its durability and ease of use.

The latter half of the 19th century saw further improvements in the design and functionality of measuring tapes. In 1864, William H. Bangs of the United States patented a tape measure that featured a spring mechanism to retract the tape into its casing automatically. This spring-return mechanism became a standard feature in measuring tapes, significantly enhancing their convenience and practicality. The incorporation of locking mechanisms, which allowed users to fix the tape in place at a desired length, further improved their functionality.

By the early 20th century, measuring tapes had become an essential tool in various industries, including construction, tailoring, and engineering. The introduction of new materials such as fiberglass and later, plastic, provided alternatives to steel tapes, offering lighter and more flexible options. These new materials were particularly beneficial in environments where metal tapes could rust or corrode. The accuracy of measuring tapes also improved with advancements in manufacturing techniques, allowing for finer gradations and more precise measurements.

One of the most significant innovations in the history of the measuring tape occurred in the mid-20th century with the invention of the self-retracting tape measure. In 1941, an American inventor named Hiram Farrand, working with the Cooper Tool Company, patented a spring-powered tape measure that could be extended and retracted with a simple push of a button. This design, which included a curved, rigid tape that could extend without bending or breaking, revolutionized the tool industry. Farrand's tape measure was compact, durable, and easy to use, quickly becoming a standard tool for professionals and amateurs alike.

The post-war era saw a surge in the popularity and variety of measuring tapes. Manufacturers began to produce tapes with various features to cater to specific needs, such as magnetic tips for metalworking, dual-sided measurements for versatility, and specialized tapes for electrical work with non-conductive materials. The integration of ergonomic designs, including comfortable grips and shock-absorbing cases, made measuring tapes even more user-friendly and durable.

As technology advanced, digital measuring tapes were introduced, providing even greater accuracy and functionality. These digital tapes often featured LCD screens that displayed measurements in multiple units, memory functions to store readings, and laser guides for precise alignment. The incorporation of Bluetooth technology allowed digital measuring tapes to connect with smartphones and tablets, enabling users to transfer measurements directly to design software or share them with colleagues instantly.

In addition to professional uses, measuring tapes also became a common household tool, essential for everyday tasks such as home improvement projects, furniture arrangement, and crafting. Their compact size, ease of use, and reliability made them a staple in toolboxes and workshops around the world. The versatility of measuring tapes extended to various hobbies and crafts, from sewing and quilting to carpentry and DIY projects, highlighting their universal appeal and necessity.

The evolution of the measuring tape also reflects broader trends in design and innovation. The shift from handcrafted tools to mass-produced items during the industrial revolution paralleled the development of standardized measurements, which were crucial for global trade and industry. The invention and refinement of the measuring tape demonstrate the importance of precision and accuracy in an increasingly complex and interconnected world.

Today, the measuring tape continues to evolve with new materials, designs, and technologies. Innovations such as bi-directional tape measures, which can be read from both sides, and tapes with high-visibility markings for low-light conditions, cater to the specific needs of modern users. The integration of sustainable materials and manufacturing processes reflects a growing awareness of environmental impact and the demand for eco-friendly products.

Chapter 30: The Origins of the Highlighter

The origins of the highlighter, a ubiquitous tool in education and professional settings, is a rich story that reflects broader developments in writing instruments, chemistry, and the evolving needs of students and professionals for more effective ways to emphasize and organize information. The highlighter's journey from concept to widespread utility spans the 20th century, intertwining advancements in ink technology, the rise of the felt-tip pen, and the educational methods that emphasize visual learning and information retention.

The concept of highlighting text is not new. Before the advent of the highlighter, individuals used various methods to emphasize important information in texts, such as underlining with pens or pencils, using different colored inks, or even marking margins with symbols. These techniques, while effective to some extent, had limitations. Underlining or writing in the margins required a steady hand and often obscured parts of the text. Colored inks could be hard to differentiate or might bleed through the paper. There was a need for a more effective and less intrusive method to make key information stand out.

The development of the highlighter is closely tied to the evolution of the felt-tip pen. The felt-tip pen, a precursor to the highlighter, was invented in the 1960s by Yukio Horie of the Tokyo Stationery Company. Horie's invention used a porous, fibrous tip made from felt, which allowed for smooth ink flow and greater control over the application of ink. This invention laid the groundwork for the creation of the highlighter. The felt-tip pen was initially used for writing and drawing but was quickly adapted for other uses due to its versatility.

The specific invention of the highlighter, however, is credited to Dr. Frank Honn, who developed the first commercially successful highlighter pen in the early 1960s while working for the Carter's Ink Company. Honn's highlighter used a water-based fluorescent ink that was both translucent and vibrant, making it ideal for marking text without obscuring it. The original highlighter, called the Hi-Liter, was introduced in 1963 and featured a chisel tip that allowed for both broad and fine strokes, making it versatile for different types of text and applications. The bright, fluorescent ink used in these early highlighters was groundbreaking because it stood out against the standard black and blue inks used in printed texts, drawing the reader's eye to the highlighted sections without making the underlying text illegible.

The introduction of the Hi-Liter revolutionized the way people interacted with texts. Students found it especially useful for studying, as it allowed them to easily mark important passages in textbooks and notes, facilitating more effective review and information retention. The highlighter also became a valuable tool in the professional world, particularly in fields that required the analysis and organization of large amounts of information, such as law, medicine, and academia.

Following the success of the Hi-Liter, other companies began to produce their own versions of the highlighter, incorporating various improvements and innovations. Different colors of fluorescent ink were developed, allowing users to categorize information by color, which further enhanced the utility of the highlighter as an organizational tool. By the 1980s, highlighters were available in a range of colors, including yellow, green, pink, blue, and orange, each providing the same level of brightness and visibility.

The highlighter's impact on education cannot be overstated. It coincided with and supported pedagogical strategies that emphasized active reading and learning. Educators encouraged students to engage with texts by highlighting key points, terms, and concepts, making the highlighter an indispensable study aid. Research in educational psychology showed that visual aids, including color-coding, helped improve memory and comprehension, lending scientific support to the widespread adoption of highlighters.

The highlighter's design also evolved over time to enhance its functionality and ease of use. Manufacturers began to experiment with different tip shapes and sizes, leading to the development of dual-tip highlighters that offered both broad and fine tips in a single pen. This versatility made it easier for users to highlight text of varying sizes and to underline or annotate with precision. The ergonomic design of highlighters also improved, with contoured grips and lightweight materials making them more comfortable to use for extended periods.

Environmental considerations also played a role in the development of highlighters. As awareness of environmental issues grew, manufacturers began to produce highlighters using non-toxic, water-based inks and recyclable materials. Some companies introduced refillable highlighters, reducing waste and appealing to environmentally conscious consumers. These innovations ensured that highlighters remained relevant and responsible in an increasingly eco-aware market.

The digital age brought new challenges and opportunities for the highlighter. With the advent of digital documents and e-readers, the traditional highlighter faced potential obsolescence. However, software developers quickly integrated digital highlighting features into word processors, PDF readers, and e-book platforms. These digital highlighters mimic the functionality of their physical counterparts, allowing users to mark and organize text electronically. This transition ensured that the core utility of the highlighter—emphasizing and organizing information—remained intact in the digital realm.

The proliferation of mobile devices and apps also expanded the highlighter's capabilities. Educational and productivity apps now offer advanced highlighting features, such as the ability to highlight text in multiple colors, add annotations, and sync highlights across devices.

These digital tools have further enhanced the efficiency and effectiveness of highlighting as a study and organizational aid.

In the context of collaborative work and remote learning, digital highlighting has become even more valuable. Tools like Google Docs and collaborative platforms offer real-time highlighting and annotation features, enabling multiple users to interact with the same document simultaneously. This capability supports collaborative learning and teamwork, allowing users to share insights and highlight important information collectively.

Despite the rise of digital tools, the traditional highlighter remains a popular and indispensable tool in many settings. The tactile experience of using a physical highlighter, the immediate visual feedback it provides, and its simplicity and reliability ensure its continued relevance. Moreover, for individuals who prefer to study and work with physical texts, the highlighter remains a trusted companion.

The evolution of the highlighter reflects broader trends in education, technology, and consumer preferences. It has adapted to changing needs and environments, maintaining its core function while embracing new possibilities. The highlighter's journey from a simple tool to a sophisticated, multi-functional aid underscores its enduring value and versatility.

Chapter 31: The Tale of the Rubber Duck

The tale of the rubber duck is a charming narrative that spans more than a century, touching upon innovations in materials, changes in manufacturing techniques, and evolving cultural attitudes towards childhood, play, and hygiene. This unassuming, yet iconic, toy has undergone a fascinating evolution from its earliest incarnations to become a beloved symbol of childhood and bath time fun.

The origins of the rubber duck can be traced back to the 19th century, a period marked by significant advancements in industrial manufacturing and the introduction of new materials. The precursor to the rubber duck was born during this era, as rubber began to be used more widely in the production of various goods. Natural rubber, derived from the latex sap of rubber trees, was first introduced to Europe in the 18th century. However, it wasn't until the invention of vulcanization by Charles Goodyear in 1839 that rubber became a durable and versatile material suitable for a wide range of products, including toys.

Early rubber toys, including ducks, were typically made from solid rubber. These toys were quite different from the rubber ducks we are familiar with today. They were heavier, less buoyant, and primarily intended for use outside of the bathtub. These early versions were more ornamental than functional and were not particularly popular as bath toys. However, as manufacturing techniques improved and the understanding of rubber's properties evolved, so did the potential for more playful and practical designs.

The transition from solid rubber to hollow, buoyant rubber ducks began in the early 20th century. Advances in rubber molding techniques allowed for the creation of hollow toys that were lighter and could float on water, making them ideal for bath time. One of the earliest patents for a floating toy was granted in 1928 to the Seiberling Latex Products Company, which produced a variety of rubber animals, including ducks. These early floating toys were relatively simple in design but marked a significant step towards the rubber duck's eventual iconic status.

The 1940s and 1950s saw the rubber duck evolve further, driven by post-World War II consumer culture and the baby boom. During this period, the toy industry experienced a boom, with increased demand for children's products, including toys for the bathtub. Rubber ducks became a staple in many households, offering a fun and safe way for children to enjoy bath time. The development of synthetic rubber and plastics during and after the war also played a crucial role in making rubber ducks more affordable and widely available. These materials allowed for more vibrant colors, detailed designs, and durable products.

One of the most significant milestones in the history of the rubber duck occurred in the 1970s with the rise of Sesame Street, a popular children's television program. In 1970, the character Ernie sang "Rubber Duckie," an ode to his beloved bath toy, on the show. The song became an instant hit, reaching number 16 on the Billboard Hot 100 chart and cementing the rubber duck's place in popular culture. This moment was pivotal in transforming the rubber duck from a simple bath toy into an enduring cultural icon. The association with Ernie and the catchy tune helped endear rubber ducks to generations of children and parents, making them a quintessential symbol of childhood.

Throughout the late 20th century, rubber ducks continued to evolve in terms of design and variety. Manufacturers experimented with different colors, sizes, and themes, creating an array of rubber ducks to appeal to diverse tastes and preferences. The classic yellow rubber duck remained the most popular, but themed ducks, such as those dressed as pirates, princesses, or animals, began to emerge. This diversification allowed rubber ducks to remain relevant and appealing in an increasingly competitive toy market.

In addition to their playful appeal, rubber ducks also became associated with safety and hygiene. Bath time is an important ritual for young children, not only for cleanliness but also for sensory development and bonding with parents. Rubber ducks, with their soft, squeezable bodies and bright colors, provide sensory stimulation and encourage imaginative play. Parents appreciated their simplicity, safety, and the way they helped make bath time a more enjoyable experience for their children.

The turn of the 21st century brought new dimensions to the tale of the rubber duck. In 2001, Dutch artist Florentijn Hofman created a series of large, inflatable rubber duck sculptures, which he called "Rubber Duck." These enormous floating installations, some as tall as 54 feet, were displayed in various cities around the world, from Sydney to Los Angeles to Hong Kong. Hofman's giant rubber ducks captured the public's imagination and highlighted the whimsical, universal appeal of the toy. His art installations played on the nostalgia and simplicity of the rubber duck, making a profound statement about childhood and joy in urban environments.

Rubber ducks also found a place in environmental and scientific discussions. In 1992, a shipping container filled with thousands of rubber ducks and other bath toys was lost at sea during a storm in the Pacific Ocean. Over the years, these toys, known as the Friendly Floatees, began to wash up on shores around the world. Oceanographers and environmentalists tracked the movements of these rubber ducks, gaining valuable insights into ocean currents and the impact of marine debris. The story of the Friendly Floatees highlighted issues of pollution and the interconnectedness of the world's oceans, adding an unexpected scientific and environmental dimension to the rubber duck's story.

The cultural significance of rubber ducks has also been recognized through various events and records. The annual Great British Duck Race, which started in 2007, involves thousands of rubber ducks racing down the River Thames, raising funds for charity. Similar events have been held in other countries, demonstrating the rubber duck's global appeal and its ability to bring people together for a good cause. In 2013, the Guinness World Record for the largest rubber duck race was set in Pittsburgh, Pennsylvania, with over 200,000 rubber ducks participating.

Today, the rubber duck continues to be a beloved and enduring toy. Its simple design and cheerful appearance have made it a timeless classic, appealing to children and adults alike. Rubber ducks are often used in marketing and branding, symbolizing fun, relaxation, and nostalgia. They have become collectibles, with enthusiasts seeking out rare and unique designs from around the world.

The manufacturing of rubber ducks has also seen advancements in recent years. Modern rubber ducks are typically made from non-toxic, phthalate-free materials, addressing concerns about the safety and environmental impact of plastic toys. Some companies have even introduced biodegradable rubber ducks, further aligning with contemporary values of sustainability and environmental responsibility.

Chapter 32: The Rise of the Ebook Reader

The rise of the ebook reader is a fascinating story that intertwines technological advancements, shifts in consumer behavior, and the evolution of the publishing industry. From its early conceptual stages to its widespread adoption, the ebook reader has fundamentally changed the way people read, distribute, and access written content. This transformation has been driven by a combination of innovations in electronic ink technology, digital content distribution, and the increasing ubiquity of internet connectivity, culminating in a profound shift in how we consume books and other textual materials.

The concept of an electronic book predates the modern ebook reader by several decades. As early as the 1940s, visionary thinkers like Vannevar Bush envisioned devices that could store and retrieve large amounts of information electronically. Bush's hypothetical "memex" device, described in his 1945 essay "As We May Think," was an early conceptual precursor to digital libraries and ebook readers. However, the technology needed to realize such a vision was not yet available.

The first tangible steps towards the development of ebook readers occurred in the 1970s and 1980s with the advent of personal computers. In 1971, Michael S. Hart launched the Project Gutenberg initiative, which aimed to digitize and archive literary works, making them freely available to the public. Project Gutenberg can be seen as the precursor to modern digital libraries and ebook distribution platforms. However, reading digital texts on early computer screens was not user-friendly, and the hardware was not portable, limiting the practicality of digital reading.

The 1990s brought significant advancements in display technology, which paved the way for more practical ebook readers. One of the key breakthroughs was the development of electronic ink (e-ink) technology. Unlike traditional LCD screens, which can cause eye strain over long periods of reading, e-ink displays mimic the appearance of ink on paper, providing a more comfortable and natural reading experience. E-ink screens are also highly energy-efficient, allowing devices to run for extended periods on a single battery charge. The first commercial e-ink display was developed by E Ink Corporation, a spin-off from the Massachusetts Institute of Technology (MIT), in the late 1990s.

Despite these technological advancements, early ebook readers struggled to gain traction. Devices such as the Rocket eBook and the SoftBook Reader, both introduced in the late 1990s, featured e-ink displays and portable designs but were hampered by limited content availability, high prices, and the lack of a standardized ebook format. Additionally, the internet infrastructure necessary to support widespread ebook distribution was still in its infancy.

The turn of the 21st century marked a turning point for ebook readers. The increasing adoption of broadband internet, combined with the growing popularity of mobile devices, created a more favorable environment for digital reading. In 2004, Sony introduced the Librie, one of the first ebook readers to use e-ink technology. The Librie offered a significant improvement in readability and battery life over earlier devices, but it still faced challenges related to content availability and digital rights management (DRM).

The true breakthrough for ebook readers came in 2007 with the launch of the Amazon Kindle. The Kindle was not the first ebook reader, but it was the first to achieve mainstream success, thanks to several key innovations. First, the Kindle featured a high-quality e-ink display that provided a paper-like reading experience. Second, Amazon integrated wireless connectivity into the device, allowing users to purchase and download books directly from the Kindle Store without needing to connect to a computer. This seamless integration of hardware, software, and content was a game-changer, making it easy for users to access a vast library of ebooks anytime, anywhere.

Amazon's extensive digital content ecosystem played a crucial role in the Kindle's success. By offering a wide selection of books, including bestsellers and exclusive titles, at competitive prices, Amazon attracted a large number of readers to the platform. The company also introduced features like the ability to adjust font sizes, highlight text, and sync reading progress across multiple devices, enhancing the overall reading experience. The Kindle's success spurred other major tech companies to enter the ebook reader market, leading to increased competition and innovation.

In 2010, Apple released the iPad, a multifunctional tablet that included an ebook reading app called iBooks. While not a dedicated ebook reader, the iPad's versatility and vibrant display attracted many users, particularly those who preferred a device that could handle a variety of multimedia content. The iPad's introduction highlighted the growing convergence of digital media and the importance of versatile, multi-use devices in the evolving digital landscape.

Competition in the ebook reader market intensified with the introduction of Barnes & Noble's Nook and Kobo's line of ebook readers. These devices offered features such as touchscreens, higher resolution displays, and enhanced connectivity options, pushing the boundaries of what ebook readers could offer. The competition also led to price reductions, making ebook readers more accessible to a broader audience.

The rise of the ebook reader was accompanied by significant changes in the publishing industry. Traditional publishers began to embrace digital formats, recognizing the potential for reaching new audiences and reducing production and distribution costs. Self-publishing platforms like Amazon's Kindle Direct Publishing (KDP) democratized the publishing process, allowing independent authors to publish and distribute their works directly to readers. This shift empowered a new generation of writers and broadened the diversity of available content.

The increasing popularity of ebooks and ebook readers also sparked debates over DRM and digital ownership. DRM technologies were implemented to prevent unauthorized copying and distribution of digital books, but they also restricted users' ability to share or transfer their purchased content. Critics argued that DRM limited consumer rights and stifled the free flow of information. Over time, some publishers and platforms began to experiment with DRM-free models, seeking a balance between protecting intellectual property and providing flexibility to readers.

As ebook readers evolved, so did the software and services associate with them. Features like dictionary look-up, translation, and annotation became standard, enhancing the reading experience and making ebook readers valuable tools for education and research. The integration of cloud storage and synchronization allowed readers to access their entire library across multiple devices, ensuring that they could pick up where they left off, regardless of the device they were using.

The rise of the ebook reader also had environmental implications. Digital books eliminated the need for paper, ink, and physical transportation, reducing the environmental footprint associated with traditional book production and distribution. However, the production and disposal of electronic devices presented new environmental challenges, prompting discussions about sustainable practices and the life cycle of digital devices.

In recent years, the ebook reader market has continued to evolve with advancements in technology and changes in consumer preferences. High-resolution displays, improved front-lighting systems, and ergonomic designs have enhanced the comfort and usability of ebook readers. Devices like the Kindle Oasis and the Kobo Forma offer premium features such as adjustable warm light, waterproofing, and larger screens, catering to avid readers who seek the best possible reading experience.

The integration of audiobooks and text-to-speech functionality has further expanded the versatility of ebook readers. Platforms like Audible, acquired by Amazon in 2008, have popularized audiobooks, allowing users to listen to their favorite books while commuting, exercising, or performing other activities. The seamless integration of ebooks and audiobooks within a single ecosystem has made it easier for readers to switch between reading and listening, depending on their preferences and circumstances.

The COVID-19 pandemic accelerated the adoption of digital reading as people sought safe and convenient ways to access books and other written content. Libraries and educational institutions expanded their digital collections and services, providing remote access to ebooks and other digital resources. This shift underscored the importance of digital literacy and the role of ebook readers in supporting lifelong learning and information access.

Chapter 33: The History of the Matchstick

The history of the matchstick is a remarkable tale of human ingenuity, scientific discovery, and the relentless pursuit of convenience and safety. This small yet indispensable tool has undergone numerous transformations since its inception, reflecting broader technological advancements and changing societal needs. From the early days of fire-making techniques to the modern safety match, the matchstick's evolution is a fascinating journey through time.

The quest for a convenient and reliable method to produce fire dates back to prehistoric times. Early humans relied on laborious methods such as striking flint stones together to create sparks or using a bow drill to generate friction and ignite dry tinder. These primitive techniques, though effective, required significant effort and skill. The development of more efficient fire-making methods became a priority as civilizations advanced and the need for controlled fire grew in importance for cooking, heating, and protection.

The earliest known form of matches can be traced back to ancient China. Around 577 AD, during the Northern and Southern Dynasties period, records describe the use of sulfur-tipped sticks to start fires. These early matches, known as "fire-inch-sticks," were created by impregnating small wooden sticks with sulfur, which would ignite when exposed to a flame or a smoldering ember. While not self-igniting, these sulfur matches represented a significant step forward in the quest for a more convenient fire-starting tool.

In the centuries that followed, various cultures experimented with different materials and methods to create more efficient matches. However, it wasn't until the 17th century that significant progress was made in Europe. The discovery of phosphorus by the German alchemist Hennig Brand in 1669 marked a turning point in the development of matches. Phosphorus, a highly reactive element, was found to ignite spontaneously when exposed to air, making it an ideal candidate for use in matches.

The first self-igniting match, known as the "phosphorus match," was invented in 1805 by French chemist Jean Chancel, who worked with the scientist Claude-Louis Berthollet. Chancel's matches consisted of small wooden splints coated with a mixture of sulfur and potassium chlorate, with the tip dipped in phosphorus. These matches could be ignited by striking them against a rough surface, but they were highly dangerous due to the volatility of white phosphorus, which is toxic and ignites easily.

Despite the dangers, phosphorus matches gained popularity in the early 19th century. They were commonly known as "lucifers" and were widely used throughout Europe. However, the safety hazards associated with white phosphorus led to numerous accidents and health issues among workers in match factories. "Phossy jaw," a debilitating condition caused by prolonged exposure to white phosphorus fumes, became a significant health concern.

In response to the dangers posed by white phosphorus matches, safer alternatives were sought. The breakthrough came in 1844 when Swedish chemist Gustaf Erik Pasch invented the safety match. Pasch's innovation involved separating the reactive chemicals used in matches to prevent accidental ignition. His safety matches consisted of wooden splints coated with sulfur and potassium chlorate on one end, and the striking surface was coated with red phosphorus, an allotrope of phosphorus that is much less reactive and non-toxic compared to white phosphorus.

The safety match design was further refined by Swedish industrialist Johan Edvard Lundström, who improved the manufacturing process and made the matches more reliable. Lundström's safety matches, produced in the town of Jönköping, quickly gained popularity and became the standard for match production. The introduction of safety matches marked a significant milestone in the history of the matchstick, greatly reducing the risks associated with match use and production.

The safety match's success was not limited to Europe. In the United States, the Diamond Match Company, founded in the late 19th century, became a major player in the match industry. The company, led by Ohio industrialist O.C. Barber, adopted the safety match technology and expanded production to meet the growing demand. The Diamond Match Company played a crucial role in popularizing safety matches in America and set new standards for quality and safety in match production.

While safety matches became the norm, the matchstick continued to evolve in terms of design and materials. The traditional wooden splints were eventually replaced by cardboard splints, which were cheaper and more environmentally friendly. The striking surface was also improved, with the addition of various chemical compounds to enhance ignition reliability and reduce the risk of accidental fires.

The 20th century saw further advancements in match production and safety. Match manufacturers introduced innovations such as waterproof matches, which could be ignited even when wet, and windproof matches, designed to withstand strong winds. These specialized matches found applications in outdoor activities, survival situations, and military use, further expanding the matchstick's versatility.

Despite the rise of modern lighters and other ignition devices, matches have remained a popular and practical tool for fire-starting. Their simplicity, reliability, and affordability make them an essential item in households, camping gear, and emergency kits. Matches are also valued for their ability to ignite a fire quickly and safely, without the need for batteries or fuel.

In addition to their practical uses, matches have also found cultural and artistic significance. Matchstick art, also known as matchstick modeling, involves creating intricate sculptures and models using matchsticks as the primary material. This unique form of art has gained a following among hobbyists and artists, who appreciate the challenge and creativity involved in transforming ordinary matchsticks into elaborate works of art.

The history of the matchstick is also intertwined with significant social and political movements. In the early 20th century, matchgirls' strikes in Britain highlighted the poor working conditions and health risks faced by match factory workers. The most notable strike occurred in 1888 when female workers at the Bryant and May match factory in London protested against low wages, long hours, and the dangers of white phosphorus exposure. The strike gained public attention and led to improved working conditions and the eventual banning of white phosphorus in match production.

Environmental concerns have also influenced the match industry. The production of matches requires large quantities of wood, leading to deforestation and habitat destruction. To address these issues, match manufacturers have increasingly turned to sustainable practices, such as using recycled materials and promoting responsible forestry management. Some companies have also introduced eco-friendly matches made from renewable resources, further reducing the environmental impact of match production.

In recent years, the matchstick has faced competition from electronic ignition devices, such as butane lighters and electric arc lighters. These modern alternatives offer convenience and reusability, reducing the need for disposable matches. However, matches continue to hold a unique place in the market due to their simplicity, reliability, and nostalgic appeal. They remain a preferred choice for certain applications, such as lighting candles, campfires, and fireplaces, where the controlled flame of a match is advantageous.

The matchstick's enduring popularity can be attributed to its timeless design and functionality. Despite the many technological advancements and changes in consumer preferences, the basic principles of the match have remained largely unchanged for over a century.

Chapter 34: The Innovation of the Barcode

The innovation of the barcode is a compelling story of technological advancement, market need, and the relentless drive for efficiency and accuracy in various industries. From its inception as a simple idea for speeding up grocery checkout lines to its widespread adoption across countless sectors, the barcode has become an indispensable tool for tracking and managing products, assets, and information. The journey of the barcode, spanning several decades, highlights the interplay between technological innovation and practical application, ultimately transforming how businesses operate and consumers interact with products.

The concept of a machine-readable code to streamline retail operations can be traced back to the late 1940s. The story begins with a graduate student named Bernard Silver at Drexel Institute of Technology in Philadelphia. Silver overheard a conversation between the dean of the university and a local grocery store owner who was seeking a more efficient way to manage inventory and speed up the checkout process. Intrigued by the challenge, Silver shared the idea with his friend, Norman Joseph Woodland. This serendipitous conversation sparked the beginning of the barcode's development.

Woodland, inspired by Morse code, initially conceived the idea of a linear code comprising varying widths of bars and spaces. He envisioned a system where data could be encoded in a pattern of lines that a machine could read optically. Woodland and Silver's early experiments involved creating a barcode using a series of straight lines. They filed a patent application for their "Classifying Apparatus and Method" in 1949, which was granted in 1952. Their design described a system that used ultraviolet light to read the encoded data, a concept that was innovative but ahead of its time in terms of the technology available.

Despite their groundbreaking work, Woodland and Silver faced significant technological limitations. The computing power and scanning technology required to implement their system effectively did not exist in the early 1950s. Consequently, their invention remained largely theoretical, with no immediate practical applications. However, the foundation they laid was crucial for future developments in barcode technology.

The barcode concept saw renewed interest in the 1960s, driven by advancements in computing and the growing need for automation in various industries. During this period, railroads and the automotive industry explored automated identification systems to improve tracking and logistics. One notable development was the KarTrak system, developed by Sylvania Electric Products, which used colored stripes to identify railroad cars. Although the system was eventually abandoned due to reliability issues, it demonstrated the potential benefits of automated identification and laid the groundwork for further innovation.

The real breakthrough for barcodes came in the late 1960s and early 1970s with the advent of optical scanning technology and the development of the Universal Product Code (UPC). In 1970, the Uniform Grocery Product Code Council (later known as the Uniform Code Council, or UCC) was formed to develop a standardized system for identifying products in the grocery industry. The council sought to create a universal coding scheme that could be used by all retailers and manufacturers, simplifying inventory management and checkout processes.

IBM, one of the companies involved in the project, played a pivotal role in developing the UPC. George J. Laurer, an engineer at IBM, was instrumental in designing the UPC symbol, which consisted of a series of black bars and white spaces of varying widths. The UPC symbol encoded a 12-digit number, with the first six digits representing the manufacturer and the next five digits identifying the specific product. The final digit was a check digit used for error detection.

The first commercial use of the UPC occurred on June 26, 1974, when a pack of Wrigley's Juicy Fruit gum was scanned at a Marsh supermarket in Troy, Ohio. This historic moment marked the beginning of the widespread adoption of barcode technology in the retail industry. The UPC system proved to be highly effective, significantly reducing checkout times and improving inventory management for retailers. As a result, barcodes quickly became a standard feature on consumer products, revolutionizing the way goods were tracked and sold.

The success of the UPC in the retail sector spurred further innovation and adoption of barcode technology across various industries. Barcodes began to be used in manufacturing, logistics, healthcare, and other sectors to improve efficiency, accuracy, and traceability. In the manufacturing industry, barcodes enabled companies to track components and finished products through the production process, reducing errors and improving quality control. In logistics, barcodes facilitated the tracking of shipments and inventory, optimizing supply chain operations and reducing costs.

One significant development in barcode technology was the introduction of the Code 39 barcode in the early 1980s. Code 39, developed by Intermec, was a more versatile alphanumeric barcode that could encode both letters and numbers. This flexibility made it suitable for a wide range of applications, from inventory management to asset tracking. Code 39 became widely adopted in various industries, further expanding the use of barcode technology.

The healthcare industry also embraced barcodes to improve patient safety and operational efficiency. Barcodes were used to label medications, medical devices, and patient records, reducing the risk of errors and ensuring accurate tracking of medical supplies. The adoption of barcodes in healthcare was driven by the need for better inventory management, compliance with regulatory requirements, and the desire to enhance patient care.

The evolution of barcode technology continued with the development of two-dimensional (2D) barcodes, such as the QR code, in the 1990s. Unlike traditional linear barcodes, which store data in a series of parallel lines, 2D barcodes store information in a matrix of squares or dots. This design allows 2D barcodes to encode much larger amounts of data in a smaller space. QR codes, developed by Denso Wave, a subsidiary of Toyota, were initially used for tracking automotive parts but quickly found applications in marketing, ticketing, and other fields due to their versatility and ease of use.

The widespread adoption of smartphones in the 2000s further boosted the popularity of 2D barcodes. Smartphones equipped with cameras and barcode scanning apps enabled consumers to scan QR codes to access product information, promotions, and online content. This integration of barcode technology with mobile devices opened up new possibilities for marketing and customer engagement, allowing businesses to interact with consumers in innovative ways.

In addition to QR codes, other types of 2D barcodes, such as Data Matrix and PDF417, have been developed for specific applications. Data Matrix codes are commonly used in manufacturing and logistics for marking small items and components, while PDF417 codes are used for encoding large amounts of data, such as boarding passes and driver's licenses. These advancements in barcode technology have expanded the range of applications and improved the efficiency and accuracy of data capture and tracking.

The innovation of the barcode has also had a profound impact on supply chain management. The ability to track products and shipments in real-time has enabled businesses to optimize inventory levels, reduce stockouts, and improve order fulfillment. Radio-frequency identification (RFID) technology, which uses radio waves to read and capture information stored on tags, has further enhanced supply chain visibility and efficiency. RFID tags can store more data than traditional barcodes and can be read from a distance without requiring line-of-sight, making them ideal for tracking items in complex supply chain environments.

The integration of barcodes and RFID technology with enterprise resource planning (ERP) systems and other business software has enabled companies to streamline operations and improve decision-making. Real-time data captured through barcodes and RFID tags can be used to monitor inventory levels, track production progress, and analyze supply chain performance. This data-driven approach has helped businesses to identify inefficiencies, reduce costs, and enhance overall operational effectiveness.

As barcode technology has evolved, so too have the standards and regulations governing its use. The development of international standards, such as those set by the International Organization for Standardization (ISO), has ensured the interoperability and compatibility of barcode systems across different countries and industries. Standardized barcodes enable global trade and commerce by providing a common language for identifying and tracking products. Organizations such as GS1, a global standards organization, have played a crucial role in developing and promoting barcode standards, including the widely used Global Trade Item Number (GTIN) and Global Location Number (GLN).

The future of barcode technology holds exciting possibilities as advancements in artificial intelligence (AI), machine learning, and the Internet of Things (IoT) continue to shape the digital landscape. AI-powered image recognition and computer vision technologies are enhancing the capabilities of barcode scanning, enabling faster and more accurate data capture. IoT devices equipped with barcode and RFID readers are being used to create smart supply chains, where products and assets can be tracked and managed in real-time.

Innovations such as blockchain technology are also being explored to improve the transparency and security of supply chains. By combining barcodes and blockchain, businesses can create immutable records of product movements and transactions, ensuring the integrity and traceability of goods from source to consumer. This integration of barcode technology with emerging digital technologies has the potential to revolutionize industries and create new opportunities for efficiency and innovation.

Chapter 35: The Story Behind the Adhesive Bandage

The adhesive bandage, a simple yet revolutionary invention, has a fascinating history that intertwines innovation, necessity, and the drive to make everyday life safer and more convenient. This ubiquitous item, found in medicine cabinets, first-aid kits, and classrooms worldwide, represents a significant advancement in wound care. Its development was not only a response to a personal need but also a reflection of broader trends in medical innovation and consumer product design. The story behind the adhesive bandage involves ingenious problem-solving, the evolution of medical practices, and the adaptation to changing societal needs.

The origin of the adhesive bandage can be traced back to the early 20th century, a period marked by rapid advancements in medical technology and hygiene practices. Prior to the invention of the adhesive bandage, treating minor wounds was a cumbersome process. Traditional methods involved using strips of cloth or gauze secured with tape or ties, which were not only inconvenient but also ineffective in providing adequate protection against infection. The need for a more efficient and user-friendly solution was evident, setting the stage for the invention of the adhesive bandage.

The credit for this groundbreaking invention goes to Earle Dickson, an employee at Johnson & Johnson, a company already renowned for its contributions to healthcare products. The story begins in 1920 when Dickson observed his wife, Josephine, struggling with frequent minor cuts and burns while performing household chores. Josephine's injuries required constant care and dressing, but the available wound care solutions were inadequate. The dressings would often slip off, and the cumbersome application process made it difficult for Josephine to manage her injuries effectively.

Motivated by the desire to help his wife, Dickson set out to create a more practical solution. Drawing on his knowledge of Johnson & Johnson's sterile gauze and surgical tape products, he devised a prototype that combined these elements into a single, easy-to-use product. Dickson took a piece of sterile gauze and placed it in the center of an adhesive strip, which he then covered with crinoline fabric to protect the adhesive until it was ready to be used. This simple yet ingenious design allowed Josephine to quickly and easily dress her wounds without assistance.

Recognizing the potential of his invention, Dickson presented his prototype to his superiors at Johnson & Johnson. The company's management was impressed by the practicality and convenience of the adhesive bandage and saw its potential as a mass-market product. In 1921, Johnson & Johnson began manufacturing and selling the first commercial adhesive bandages under the brand name "Band-Aid." These early versions were handmade and came in individual packages, which was a labor-intensive process that limited production capacity.

Despite initial production challenges, the Band-Aid adhesive bandage quickly gained popularity due to its simplicity and effectiveness. The product's success can be attributed to several key factors. First, the adhesive bandage addressed a common problem faced by many households: the need for a quick and reliable way to treat minor injuries. Second, the Band-Aid was user-friendly and could be applied by anyone, without the need for medical training. This accessibility made it an ideal product for families, schools, and workplaces.

As demand for the Band-Aid grew, Johnson & Johnson invested in mechanizing the production process to increase output and reduce costs. By the mid-1920s, the company had developed automated machinery capable of producing adhesive bandages in large quantities. This innovation not only improved production efficiency but also allowed for the standardization of product quality, ensuring that every Band-Aid met the same high standards of effectiveness and safety.

The success of the Band-Aid adhesive bandage also prompted Johnson & Johnson to explore new variations and improvements to meet the evolving needs of consumers. In the 1930s, the company introduced the first sterilized Band-Aids, which were individually sealed in cellophane wrappers to maintain their sterility until use. This development was particularly important for preventing infections and ensuring the safety of wound care products. Sterilized Band-Aids became the industry standard, further cementing the product's reputation for reliability and quality.

The outbreak of World War II in the 1940s created new challenges and opportunities for the adhesive bandage. The war effort required vast quantities of medical supplies, including adhesive bandages, to treat wounded soldiers on the battlefield. Johnson & Johnson ramped up production to meet the military's needs, supplying millions of Band-Aids to the armed forces. The adhesive bandage's effectiveness in treating minor wounds and preventing infections made it an essential item in military first-aid kits, and its use in the field highlighted its value in emergency situations.

The post-war period saw a boom in consumer goods and healthcare products, with the adhesive bandage becoming a staple in households across the United States and beyond. Johnson & Johnson continued to innovate, introducing new features and designs to enhance the product's appeal. In the 1950s, the company launched the first decorative Band-Aids, featuring colorful prints and cartoon characters. These fun and playful designs were particularly popular with children, making the process of treating minor injuries less intimidating and more engaging for young patients.

The 1960s and 1970s witnessed further advancements in adhesive bandage technology and design. Johnson & Johnson introduced flexible fabric Band-Aids, which provided greater comfort and mobility for users. These bandages were designed to stretch and conform to the contours of the body, making them ideal for use on joints and other areas that required flexibility. Additionally, the company developed waterproof Band-Aids, which offered protection against water and moisture, allowing users to continue their daily activities without worrying about their bandages coming off.

The adhesive bandage's evolution continued into the late 20th and early 21st centuries, with ongoing improvements in materials, adhesives, and packaging. Modern Band-Aids are made from advanced materials that provide superior adhesion, breathability, and comfort. Silicone adhesives, for example, offer gentle and secure adhesion, reducing the risk of skin irritation and making bandages easier to remove without causing pain. Innovations in packaging, such as easy-open wrappers and individually sealed bandages, have also enhanced the convenience and usability of the product.

In addition to traditional adhesive bandages, the market has seen the introduction of specialized products designed for specific medical needs. Antibacterial Band-Aids, for instance, contain antiseptic agents that help prevent infections and promote faster healing. Hydrocolloid bandages, which create a moist healing environment, are used for treating blisters, burns, and other types of wounds that benefit from moisture retention. These specialized products reflect the ongoing commitment of manufacturers to meet diverse consumer needs and provide effective wound care solutions.

The adhesive bandage has also found applications beyond traditional wound care. In recent years, wearable technology has emerged as a growing field, with researchers developing adhesive bandages that incorporate sensors and electronics for monitoring health and delivering medication. These smart bandages have the potential to revolutionize healthcare by providing real-time data on wound healing, detecting infections, and administering precise doses of medication directly to the wound site. The integration of technology into adhesive bandages represents a new frontier in wound care, combining the convenience of traditional bandages with the capabilities of advanced medical devices.

The story behind the adhesive bandage is not just about the product itself but also about the impact it has had on healthcare, consumer behavior, and even cultural trends. The Band-Aid brand, in particular, has become synonymous with adhesive bandages, a testament to its enduring popularity and widespread recognition. The brand's name has entered the lexicon as a generic term for adhesive bandages, reflecting its cultural significance and the deep connection consumers have with the product.

Throughout its history, the adhesive bandage has been more than just a practical tool; it has also been a symbol of care and compassion. For many people, the act of applying a Band-Aid is a gesture of comfort and protection, whether it's a parent tending to a child's scraped knee or a caregiver treating a patient's wound. This emotional connection underscores the adhesive bandage's role in everyday life and its importance as a means of providing immediate and effective care for minor injuries.

Chapter 36: The Rise of the Flashlight

The rise of the flashlight is a fascinating tale of technological evolution, practical necessity, and human ingenuity. From the dim glow of early handheld torches to the powerful beams of modern LED flashlights, this story spans over a century and encompasses numerous innovations that have transformed the way we illuminate our surroundings. The journey of the flashlight reflects broader trends in scientific discovery, industrial design, and the relentless pursuit of improving everyday tools for human convenience and safety.

The concept of a portable light source predates the invention of the flashlight, with early attempts to create handheld illumination dating back to ancient times. In the absence of electricity, people relied on oil lamps, candles, and torches to provide light in the dark. These rudimentary tools were far from ideal, offering limited illumination, posing fire hazards, and being impractical for many applications. The need for a safer, more reliable, and portable source of light was evident, setting the stage for the invention of the flashlight.

The development of the flashlight began in earnest in the late 19th century, coinciding with significant advancements in electrical technology. The invention of the electric battery and the incandescent light bulb were crucial milestones that paved the way for portable electric lighting. In 1800, Italian physicist Alessandro Volta invented the voltaic pile, the first true battery, which provided a steady electric current. This invention was followed by the development of various types of batteries, including the dry cell battery, which played a pivotal role in the creation of the flashlight.

The dry cell battery, invented by German scientist Carl Gassner in 1886, was a major breakthrough. Unlike earlier batteries, which were prone to leakage and required careful handling, the dry cell battery was sealed and used a paste electrolyte instead of a liquid. This design made it more durable, portable, and suitable for a wide range of applications.

The introduction of the dry cell battery provided a reliable power source for portable electric devices, including the flashlight.

The incandescent light bulb, invented by Thomas Edison in 1879, was another key component in the development of the flashlight. Edison's light bulb used a carbon filament enclosed in a glass bulb, which produced light when an electric current passed through it. This invention revolutionized indoor lighting and laid the foundation for electric illumination. The challenge, however, was to miniaturize the light bulb and battery to create a portable light source that could be easily carried and used.

The first practical flashlight was invented by David Misell, a British inventor, in 1899. Misell, who later moved to the United States, received a patent for his invention on January 10, 1899. His design featured a tubular casing, a simple on-off switch, and a light bulb powered by three D-cell batteries. Misell's flashlight was manufactured by the American Electrical Novelty and Manufacturing Company, which was later renamed Eveready. Although Misell's early flashlights were rudimentary by modern standards, they represented a significant leap forward in portable lighting technology.

Early flashlights, often called "electric hand torches," were limited by the technology of the time. The incandescent bulbs used in these flashlights were inefficient, producing a dim light and consuming a lot of battery power. As a result, the batteries had a short lifespan, and the light output was weak. Despite these limitations, the flashlight quickly gained popularity due to its convenience and safety compared to traditional sources of light like candles and oil lamps.

The early 20th century saw continuous improvements in flashlight design and performance. Innovations in battery technology, such as the introduction of more efficient alkaline batteries, extended the operational life of flashlights. The development of tungsten filament bulbs, which were brighter and more durable than carbon filaments, significantly improved the brightness and reliability of flashlights.

These advancements made flashlights more practical and widely accessible to consumers.

During this period, the flashlight began to find applications beyond household use. It became an essential tool for law enforcement, military personnel, and outdoor enthusiasts. The ability to carry a portable light source that could be easily activated and directed made flashlights invaluable in various situations, from nighttime patrols to emergency repairs. The military, in particular, recognized the importance of reliable portable lighting, leading to the development of specialized flashlights for use in combat and other demanding environments.

The mid-20th century marked a significant turning point in the evolution of the flashlight with the advent of new materials and manufacturing techniques. The introduction of plastic casings replaced the earlier metal ones, making flashlights lighter, more durable, and resistant to corrosion. This shift also allowed for greater design flexibility, resulting in a wide range of shapes and sizes tailored to different uses. Waterproof and shock-resistant models were developed for outdoor and industrial applications, further expanding the versatility of the flashlight.

One of the most significant advancements in flashlight technology occurred in the latter half of the 20th century with the development of light-emitting diodes (LEDs). LEDs, which convert electrical energy directly into light, offered numerous advantages over traditional incandescent bulbs. They were more energy-efficient, had a longer lifespan, and were more durable, making them ideal for use in flashlights. The first practical LED flashlight was introduced in the early 1990s, marking the beginning of a new era in portable lighting.

The adoption of LED technology revolutionized the flashlight industry. LED flashlights produced a much brighter and more focused beam of light while consuming less power, significantly extending battery life. The compact size of LEDs also allowed for the design of smaller, lighter, and more portable flashlights. These improvements made LED flashlights the preferred choice for a wide range of applications, from everyday use to professional and emergency situations.

The rise of LED flashlights was accompanied by other technological innovations that further enhanced their functionality and performance. Rechargeable batteries, such as lithium-ion batteries, became more common, providing longer operational times and reducing the need for disposable batteries. Advances in optics and reflector technology improved the focus and intensity of the light beam, allowing flashlights to illuminate objects at greater distances with greater precision.

The integration of digital technology into flashlights brought additional features and capabilities. Many modern flashlights are equipped with multiple brightness settings, strobe functions, and programmable modes, allowing users to customize the light output for different situations. Some models include built-in sensors that adjust the brightness automatically based on ambient light conditions or the distance to the illuminated object. These smart features enhance the usability and versatility of flashlights, making them more adaptable to a variety of tasks.

The design of flashlights has also evolved to meet the specific needs of different users. Tactical flashlights, for example, are designed for law enforcement and military use, featuring rugged construction, powerful beams, and additional features like strike bezels for self-defense. Headlamps, which free up the user's hands, have become popular among outdoor enthusiasts, hikers, and workers in dark or confined spaces. Keychain flashlights and penlights offer ultra-portable options for everyday carry, ensuring that a reliable light source is always within reach.

In recent years, the rise of portable solar technology has led to the development of solar-powered flashlights. These environmentally friendly devices use photovoltaic cells to charge an internal battery during the day, providing a renewable source of energy for nighttime illumination. Solar-powered flashlights are particularly valuable in off-grid and emergency situations, where access to conventional power sources may be limited.

The flashlight's role in emergency preparedness has been well-established over the years. Whether during natural disasters, power outages, or roadside emergencies, having a reliable flashlight can be a critical factor in ensuring safety and finding one's way in the dark. Emergency flashlights often come with additional features like built-in radios, sirens, and USB ports for charging other devices, making them versatile tools for crisis situations.

The cultural impact of the flashlight is also noteworthy. It has become a symbol of preparedness, self-reliance, and exploration. The flashlight's role in horror and adventure genres, from campfire stories to movies and literature, underscores its significance in the human psyche as a beacon of light in the darkness. It represents not only a practical tool but also a metaphor for hope, safety, and the human spirit's quest for knowledge and discovery.

Chapter 37: The Evolution of the Remote Control

The remote control is a ubiquitous device today, found in nearly every household, but its journey to becoming an essential part of modern life is both fascinating and complex. The concept of remote-control technology dates back to the late 19th century, although its applications were initially far removed from the conveniences we associate with it today. The evolution of the remote control is a story that intertwines with the advancements in radio, television, and other electronic devices, reflecting broader technological and social changes over more than a century.

In the late 1800s, Nikola Tesla, a pioneer in electrical engineering, introduced the idea of using radio waves to control devices remotely. In 1898, Tesla demonstrated a radio-controlled boat at Madison Square Garden, which he called a "teleautomaton." This early application of remote-control technology was groundbreaking but largely experimental and did not find immediate practical use. Nevertheless, Tesla's work laid the groundwork for future developments.

The next significant milestone came in the early 20th century with the development of the first remote controls for military purposes. During World War I, radio-controlled torpedoes and other unmanned devices were developed, showcasing the strategic importance of remote-control technology. These early devices were rudimentary and primarily operated through radio signals. The interwar period and World War II saw further advancements, with the development of more sophisticated remote-controlled weapons and surveillance systems.

After World War II, remote control technology began to find its way into consumer electronics, marking a significant shift from military to domestic applications. One of the first commercially successful remote controls for consumer use was developed by Zenith Radio Corporation in the 1950s. This device, known as the "Lazy Bones," was connected to the television by a bulky cable and allowed users to change channels and adjust the volume from a distance. While the Lazy Bones was a significant innovation, the cumbersome cable limited its convenience and appeal.

In 1955, Zenith introduced the "Flash-Matic," the first wireless television remote control. The Flash-Matic used visible light to transmit signals to the TV. Users would point the remote at photocells placed in the corners of the television screen to control functions. Although revolutionary, the Flash-Matic had its drawbacks, such as the potential for sunlight or other light sources to interfere with its operation. Despite these limitations, the Flash-Matic marked a critical step towards more practical wireless remote controls.

The next major breakthrough came in 1956 with the introduction of the "Zenith Space Command," a remote control that utilized ultrasonic sound waves. Developed by Dr. Robert Adler, this device eliminated the problems associated with light interference. The Space Command remote featured metal rods that produced high-frequency sound waves when struck by small hammers inside the remote. These sound waves were picked up by microphones in the television, allowing users to control the device. The ultrasonic remote was highly successful and became the standard for the next two decades.

In the 1970s, remote control technology took another leap forward with the advent of infrared (IR) remote controls. These devices used infrared light to transmit signals, which were less susceptible to interference than previous technologies. The first IR remote control for home use was introduced by Magnavox in 1974. Infrared remotes quickly gained popularity due to their reliability, ease of use, and the ability to control multiple functions on electronic devices. By the 1980s, IR remotes had become the industry standard for televisions, VCRs, and other home entertainment systems.

The 1980s and 1990s saw further refinements in remote control technology. Remotes became more compact and sophisticated, incorporating features such as programmable buttons and the ability to control multiple devices. The rise of home entertainment systems with numerous components, such as TVs, VCRs, DVD players, and audio receivers, led to the development of universal remote controls. These devices could be programmed to operate a variety of different brands and models, reducing the clutter of multiple remotes and enhancing user convenience.

As digital technology advanced in the late 20th and early 21st centuries, remote controls continued to evolve. The integration of microprocessors and digital signal processing allowed for even more functionality and customization. Remotes began to feature LCD screens, touchpads, and voice recognition capabilities. The advent of smart home technology further expanded the role of remote controls, enabling users to manage not just entertainment devices but also lighting, thermostats, security systems, and more from a single device.

The proliferation of smartphones and tablets in the 2000s introduced a new paradigm for remote control technology. Many modern electronic devices, including smart TVs and streaming media players, can be controlled via mobile apps, offering a more intuitive and interactive user experience. These apps often provide additional features, such as on-screen keyboards for easier text input and the ability to stream content directly from the mobile device to the television.

Voice-controlled remotes represent one of the latest advancements in the evolution of remote controls. Devices like Amazon Echo and Google Home allow users to control their smart home ecosystems through voice commands. Similarly, many smart TVs and streaming devices now come with remotes that feature built-in microphones and voice assistants, such as Amazon Alexa, Google Assistant, or Apple's

Siri. This technology not only simplifies the user experience but also makes it more accessible for individuals with disabilities.

In recent years, gesture-based controls and wearable technology have begun to emerge as potential innovations in remote control technology. Gesture-based controls use cameras and sensors to detect hand movements and translate them into commands, eliminating the need for physical remotes altogether. Wearable devices, such as smartwatches and fitness trackers, can also serve as remote controls, allowing users to manage their electronic devices with a simple tap or swipe on their wrist.

As technology continues to advance, the future of remote controls promises even more exciting developments. With the ongoing rise of artificial intelligence, machine learning, and the Internet of Things (IoT), we can expect remote control technology to become even more intelligent, intuitive, and integrated into our lives. Whether through voice, gestures, or other yet-to-be-imagined interfaces, the remote controls of the future will likely continue to redefine our relationship with the devices that surround us.

Chapter 38: The Journey of the Desk Calendar

The desk calendar, a seemingly simple yet profoundly useful tool, has a long and intricate history that reflects the evolution of human timekeeping, organizational needs, and technological advancements. The journey of the desk calendar from its ancient origins to its modern incarnations involves a fascinating interplay of cultural, scientific, and industrial developments over millennia.

The origins of the desk calendar can be traced back to the earliest attempts by human societies to keep track of time. Ancient civilizations, such as the Egyptians, Sumerians, and Mayans, developed sophisticated calendrical systems based on astronomical observations. The Egyptians, for instance, devised a solar calendar around 3000 BCE, which consisted of 365 days divided into 12 months. This early form of a calendar laid the foundation for more complex timekeeping systems that would emerge later.

In ancient Rome, the Julian calendar, introduced by Julius Caesar in 45 BCE, was a significant advancement. It standardized the length of the year at 365.25 days, incorporating a leap year every four years. This reform aimed to align the calendar year with the solar year more accurately. The Julian calendar remained in use for over a millennium and influenced the development of calendars in various cultures. During the Roman era, public calendars were often displayed in forums and other communal spaces, allowing people to keep track of important dates and events.

The Middle Ages saw further refinements in calendrical systems, particularly within the context of the Christian Church. The need to determine the dates of religious observances, such as Easter, led to the creation of ecclesiastical calendars. Monasteries and churches began producing manuscript calendars, which not only marked religious holidays but also agricultural cycles and local festivals. These early manuscript calendars can be seen as precursors to the desk calendar, serving both practical and ceremonial purposes.

The invention of the printing press by Johannes Gutenberg in the mid-15th century revolutionized the production of calendars. Printed calendars became more widely available and affordable, reaching a broader audience. The first printed calendars were wall calendars or almanacs, which included a wealth of information such as astronomical data, weather forecasts, and agricultural advice. Almanacs were particularly popular in rural areas where they served as essential tools for farmers.

By the 18th century, the industrial revolution had brought about significant changes in manufacturing and commerce. This period saw the rise of the modern office environment, which created a demand for more practical and accessible forms of timekeeping. The desk calendar emerged as a convenient solution, offering a compact and easily referenced tool for tracking dates and appointments. Early desk calendars were often simple, consisting of a single sheet of paper with a grid of dates.

The 19th century saw the desk calendar become more sophisticated and varied in its design. Innovations in printing technology allowed for greater detail and customization. Desk calendars began to feature not only the days of the month but also additional information such as phases of the moon, tide tables, and notable events. Businesses recognized the promotional potential of desk calendars, and it became common for companies to distribute branded calendars to clients and customers.

One of the significant developments in the history of the desk calendar was the introduction of the perpetual calendar in the late 19th and early 20th centuries. Perpetual calendars were designed to be reusable year after year. They typically consisted of a series of rotating discs or sliding panels that could be adjusted to display the correct dates for any given month and year. These ingenious devices were popular both as practical tools and as decorative objects.

The 20th century saw further innovations in the design and functionality of desk calendars. The advent of mass production techniques and the widespread availability of affordable paper and printing services led to an explosion in the variety of desk calendars available. Calendars became more personalized, with options to add photographs, inspirational quotes, and custom artwork. The introduction of spiral binding and tear-off sheets added convenience, allowing users to easily flip through months or remove outdated pages.

With the rise of the corporate office culture in the mid-20th century, desk calendars became an integral part of the workspace. They were not only practical tools for scheduling meetings and deadlines but also served as a means of personal expression. Employees often chose desk calendars that reflected their interests, whether it be scenic landscapes, famous artworks, or humorous cartoons. The desk calendar also became a popular corporate gift, with businesses giving branded calendars to clients and employees as a form of appreciation and marketing.

The digital revolution of the late 20th and early 21st centuries introduced new forms of timekeeping and organization. The development of personal computers, electronic organizers, and eventually smartphones and tablets provided digital alternatives to the traditional desk calendar. Digital calendars offered numerous advantages, including automated reminders, the ability to sync across multiple devices, and easy sharing of schedules with others. Despite these advancements, the desk calendar has persisted as a beloved and practical tool, often used in conjunction with digital calendars for a more comprehensive approach to time management.

In the 21st century, the desk calendar has continued to evolve, adapting to changing technologies and aesthetic preferences. One notable trend has been the resurgence of interest in analog and tactile objects in an increasingly digital world. Many people appreciate the tangible nature of a physical desk calendar, enjoying the act of writing down appointments and the visual appeal of a well-designed calendar on their desk. This trend has been reflected in the popularity of artisanal and customizable desk calendars, often featuring high-quality materials and unique designs.

Another contemporary development is the integration of sustainability into desk calendar production. As environmental awareness has grown, so too has the demand for eco-friendly products. Many manufacturers now offer desk calendars made from recycled paper and other sustainable materials. Some companies also incorporate philanthropic initiatives, such as planting a tree for every calendar sold or donating a portion of profits to environmental causes.

Today, the desk calendar remains a versatile and valued tool, available in an array of formats to suit different tastes and requirements. Whether as a functional office accessory, a personalized gift, or a statement of style, the desk calendar continues to hold a special place in our homes and workplaces. As we move forward into an increasingly interconnected and digital future, it is likely that the desk calendar will continue to evolve, blending tradition with innovation to meet the needs of future generations.

Chapter 39: The Development of the Plastic Straw

The plastic straw, a small yet highly significant object in the history of modern convenience and environmental discourse, has a fascinating development story. From its early predecessors to its widespread adoption and eventual scrutiny, the evolution of the plastic straw reflects broader societal trends, technological advancements, and changing attitudes toward single-use plastics and sustainability.

The story begins long before the invention of plastic. The concept of the straw itself dates back thousands of years. The earliest known straws were used by the ancient Sumerians around 3000 BCE. These straws were made from gold and lapis lazuli and were used primarily for drinking beer, which often contained sediment. The straws allowed drinkers to avoid consuming the solid particles. The Sumerians' invention indicates an early understanding of the practicality and convenience that straws could offer.

Throughout history, various cultures utilized natural materials to create drinking straws. For instance, rye grass straws became popular in the 19th century in America. These straws were simple, biodegradable, and cheap to produce. However, they had their drawbacks. Rye grass straws often imparted an undesirable taste to beverages and would become soggy and fall apart after a short time in liquid.

The shortcomings of natural straws led to the quest for a more durable and practical solution. In 1888, Marvin Stone, an American inventor, patented the first paper drinking straw. Stone was inspired to create a better straw while drinking a mint julep on a hot summer day. He found that the rye grass straws of the time were ruining the flavor of his drink. Stone's innovation involved winding a strip of paper around a pencil to form a thin tube, which he then coated with paraffin wax to make it waterproof. This early paper straw was a significant improvement over its predecessors and quickly gained popularity.

The paper straw remained the standard for several decades, but the advent of new materials in the mid-20th century brought about a major shift. The development of plastic polymers in the early 1900s revolutionized many industries, including food and beverage. Plastic offered several advantages over paper and other natural materials: it was durable, flexible, inexpensive to produce, and could be easily molded into various shapes. These properties made plastic an ideal material for manufacturing straws.

In the 1960s, the plastic straw as we know it today began to emerge. The availability of affordable, mass-produced plastic materials led to the widespread adoption of plastic straws in restaurants, fast-food chains, and homes. These early plastic straws were typically made from polyethylene, a versatile and widely used plastic polymer. They were available in various colors and sizes, catering to different beverages and consumer preferences.

The rise of the plastic straw coincided with the growth of the fast-food industry and the culture of convenience that characterized post-World War II America. Plastic straws became a symbol of modernity and efficiency, perfectly suited to the fast-paced lifestyle of the era. They were cheap, disposable, and provided a hygienic way to consume beverages, making them particularly appealing to the food service industry. By the 1980s, plastic straws were ubiquitous, found in virtually every restaurant, cafe, and household.

One of the significant innovations in the development of plastic straws was the introduction of the flexible, or "bendy," straw. This design was invented in the 1930s by Joseph Friedman, who was inspired by watching his young daughter struggle to drink from a straight straw. Friedman inserted a screw into a straw and wrapped dental floss around it to create ridges. When the screw was removed, the straw could bend without breaking. Although Friedman's flexible straw was initially made from paper, the concept was later adapted for plastic straws, adding to their versatility and popularity.

Despite their convenience, plastic straws began to draw scrutiny as environmental awareness grew in the late 20th and early 21st centuries. The very properties that made plastic straws appealing—durability and disposability—also made them problematic from an environmental perspective. Unlike paper or natural materials, plastic does not biodegrade easily. Instead, it breaks down into smaller and smaller pieces, known as microplastics, which persist in the environment for hundreds of years.

The environmental impact of plastic pollution became a major concern, particularly in marine ecosystems. Studies and reports highlighted the detrimental effects of plastic waste on wildlife, with images of sea turtles, seabirds, and marine mammals harmed by plastic straws becoming emblematic of the broader plastic pollution crisis. It was estimated that millions of plastic straws were being discarded daily, contributing to the growing problem of oceanic plastic waste.

The environmental movement against single-use plastics gained significant momentum in the 2010s. Activists, researchers, and concerned citizens began advocating for reductions in plastic straw usage as part of broader efforts to address plastic pollution. Social media campaigns, such as the "Strawless Ocean" initiative, raised awareness about the environmental impact of plastic straws and encouraged individuals and businesses to seek alternatives.

In response to growing public concern and activism, many businesses and municipalities began to take action. Major corporations, including Starbucks, McDonald's, and numerous hotel chains, announced plans to phase out plastic straws in favor of more sustainable alternatives. Cities and countries around the world enacted bans or restrictions on single-use plastics, including straws. For instance, Seattle became the first major U.S. city to ban plastic straws and utensils in 2018, a move that was followed by similar legislation in other cities and states.

The push to reduce plastic straw usage led to a resurgence in the development and adoption of alternative materials. Paper straws made a comeback, now produced with improved durability and eco-friendly coatings. Biodegradable and compostable straws made from materials such as PLA (polylactic acid), a bioplastic derived from renewable resources like corn starch, became increasingly popular. Other innovative alternatives included straws made from bamboo, stainless steel, glass, and even edible materials like pasta and rice.

The movement against plastic straws also sparked innovation in straw design. Companies and entrepreneurs explored new ways to make reusable straws more convenient and appealing to consumers. Collapsible straws, which could be folded and stored in small cases for easy transport, gained popularity. Similarly, telescopic straws that could be extended and retracted offered a practical solution for on-the-go use.

The development of the plastic straw and its subsequent environmental impact highlight the complex interplay between technological advancement and sustainability. While plastic straws provided unprecedented convenience and became a staple of modern consumer culture, their environmental consequences have prompted a reevaluation of our reliance on single-use plastics. The journey of the plastic straw serves as a case study in the broader challenges and opportunities associated with balancing innovation and environmental responsibility.

Chapter 40: The Mystery of the Clothespin

The clothespin, a humble yet ingenious invention, has played a crucial role in everyday life for centuries. Its evolution, design variations, and cultural significance reveal a fascinating narrative that intertwines with the history of domestic chores, technological innovation, and even artistic expression. The journey of the clothespin from rudimentary tools to modern-day convenience objects offers insights into the ingenuity of human design and the shifting dynamics of household labor.

The origins of the clothespin can be traced back to ancient times when people first began to wash and dry their clothing. Early methods for drying clothes involved draping them over bushes, rocks, or primitive clotheslines made from natural materials such as vines or animal sinew. These methods were effective but often left clothes susceptible to wind and weather, necessitating the development of tools to secure them more reliably.

The precursor to the modern clothespin appeared in various forms across different cultures. In ancient Rome, for example, clothes were often secured to drying racks with simple wooden pegs. These early devices lacked the sophistication of modern clothespins but served the essential purpose of preventing clothing from blowing away. Similar tools were likely used in other ancient societies, though detailed records are sparse.

The clothespin as we recognize it today began to take shape in the early 19th century. The Industrial Revolution brought about significant advancements in manufacturing and domestic life, leading to the invention of more practical and efficient household tools. The first known patent for a spring-loaded clothespin was filed in 1853 by David M. Smith, a prolific inventor from Springfield, Vermont.

Smith's design featured two wooden arms joined by a fulcrum and a coiled metal spring, allowing the clothespin to grip clothing firmly and securely.

Smith's invention represented a significant improvement over earlier designs, which often consisted of a single piece of wood split down the middle. The spring mechanism not only provided a stronger grip but also made the clothespin easier to use. This basic design has remained largely unchanged for over a century, testifying to its simplicity and effectiveness.

Following Smith's innovation, the clothespin underwent various refinements and adaptations. In 1887, Solon E. Moore introduced a design with a separate coil spring, which became the standard for clothespins moving forward. Moore's version, often referred to as the "spring clothespin," featured a more durable and reliable mechanism that improved the overall functionality and lifespan of the tool. This design quickly gained popularity and became a staple in households across America and beyond.

The mass production of clothespins was facilitated by advancements in woodworking and metalworking technologies. Factories began to produce clothespins in large quantities, making them affordable and accessible to a broader population. The widespread availability of clothespins contributed to the standardization of laundry practices and improved the efficiency of domestic chores.

The cultural significance of the clothespin extends beyond its practical utility. In many societies, the act of hanging laundry has been imbued with social and communal aspects. In rural and urban settings alike, the sight of clotheslines filled with drying garments has been a common and comforting scene, symbolizing domesticity and the rhythms of daily life. The clothespin, as a central component of this ritual, has thus played a role in shaping cultural norms and practices around laundry.

In the mid-20th century, the advent of automatic clothes dryers began to change the landscape of laundry practices. While these appliances offered convenience and efficiency, they also reduced the reliance on traditional clotheslines and clothespins. Despite this shift, clothespins have remained relevant, particularly in regions where outdoor drying is still preferred due to economic, environmental, or cultural reasons.

The environmental movement of the late 20th and early 21st centuries has contributed to a renewed appreciation for air drying clothes. Concerns about energy consumption, carbon footprints, and the environmental impact of household appliances have led many people to reconsider traditional methods of drying laundry. As a result, clothespins have experienced a resurgence in popularity, especially among environmentally conscious consumers.

The design of clothespins has continued to evolve in response to changing needs and preferences. Modern clothespins are made from a variety of materials, including plastic, metal, and wood. Each material offers distinct advantages: plastic clothespins are lightweight and resistant to moisture, metal clothespins are durable and strong, and wooden clothespins are aesthetically pleasing and biodegradable. Some contemporary designs incorporate additional features, such as UV protection or ergonomic grips, to enhance their functionality and user experience.

The cultural impact of the clothespin extends into the realm of art and design. Artists and designers have explored the clothespin as a subject and medium, creating works that celebrate its simplicity and utility. For example, in 1976, artist Claes Oldenburg created a monumental clothespin sculpture in Philadelphia, blending everyday objects with a sense of whimsy and grandeur. This iconic artwork underscores the cultural resonance of the clothespin and its ability to inspire creativity and reflection.

In addition to its artistic significance, the clothespin has also been a symbol of innovation and problem-solving. The simplicity of its design, combined with its effectiveness, has made it a model of functional elegance. The clothespin's enduring relevance speaks to the ingenuity of its inventors and the adaptability of its design over time.

In recent years, the clothespin has also found new applications beyond its traditional role in laundry. It's simple yet effective mechanism has made it a versatile tool for various uses, such as organizing cables, sealing food bags, and crafting. This adaptability has further cemented its place in the pantheon of useful household items.

The clothespin's journey from ancient drying tools to modern convenience objects reflects broader trends in technology, culture, and domestic life. Its evolution has been shaped by the interplay of innovation, practicality, and cultural values, highlighting the ways in which simple tools can profoundly impact daily routines and societal practices. The enduring relevance of the clothespin underscores the importance of thoughtful design and the potential for even the most unassuming objects to inspire and adapt over time.

Chapter 41: The Evolution of the Shoe Polish

The evolution of shoe polish is a fascinating journey through history, reflecting changes in materials, technology, and cultural practices. The story begins in ancient times and continues into the modern era, showcasing how this seemingly mundane product has developed into a sophisticated industry catering to diverse needs.

In ancient civilizations, such as Egypt, Greece, and Rome, footwear was typically made from leather, which required regular maintenance to remain supple and durable. Early forms of shoe polish likely consisted of natural oils and animal fats. These substances were used not only to protect the leather from drying out and cracking but also to enhance its appearance. In Egypt, for example, records indicate the use of castor oil for this purpose, while the Romans employed a variety of natural oils and waxes.

The Middle Ages saw continued use of natural oils and fats, but there was little in the way of specialized shoe polish products. Leather shoes and boots were considered valuable possessions, and their care was an essential part of maintaining one's wardrobe. This period also saw the rise of guilds and craftsmen who specialized in leatherworking, including the maintenance and repair of footwear. These artisans would have had their own recipes and methods for preserving leather, often passed down through generations.

The Renaissance brought about significant advancements in many areas, including trade and commerce, which facilitated the exchange of materials and ideas. The increased availability of exotic ingredients, such as beeswax, lanolin, and tallow, allowed for more sophisticated formulations. These ingredients were blended with natural dyes and other substances to create early versions of what we would now recognize as shoe polish. The focus was not only on preserving the leather but also on enhancing its color and shine.

The 18th and 19th centuries marked the beginning of the industrial era, which had a profound impact on the production and availability of shoe polish. The rise of factories and mass production techniques enabled the creation of standardized products that could be distributed widely. One of the earliest commercially successful shoe polishes was "Day & Martin," established in London in the early 1800s. Their polish, which used a combination of lanolin, beeswax, and dyes, became highly popular and set the stage for the modern shoe polish industry.

The development of modern chemistry in the late 19th and early 20th centuries led to significant advancements in shoe polish formulations. Synthetic dyes and new chemical compounds allowed for more effective and longer-lasting products. This period also saw the rise of brand names that would become synonymous with shoe care. One notable example is "Kiwi," which was founded in Australia in 1906 by William Ramsay. The company's success can be attributed to its innovative formula, which included a blend of waxes and solvents that provided a superior shine and protective layer.

World War I and World War II played crucial roles in the evolution of shoe polish. The military required durable and easy-to-use products to maintain soldiers' footwear under harsh conditions. This need drove innovation in packaging and formulation. Compact tins and liquid shoe polishes became standard, allowing soldiers to quickly and effectively polish their boots. The focus on durability and ease of application influenced civilian products as well, leading to the widespread adoption of these new formulations.

Post-war prosperity and the rise of consumer culture in the mid-20th century brought further changes to the shoe polish industry. Marketing and advertising became crucial components of business strategy, with brands emphasizing the aesthetic benefits of their products. The idea that well-polished shoes were a sign of professionalism and social status took hold, driving demand for high-quality shoe polish. This era also saw diversification in product offerings, including polishes specifically designed for different types of leather and colors.

The late 20th and early 21st centuries have seen a growing awareness of environmental and health concerns associated with traditional shoe polish ingredients. Many conventional polishes contain solvents and chemicals that can be harmful to both users and the environment. In response, there has been a significant shift towards eco-friendly and non-toxic formulations. Brands have developed polishes made from natural and biodegradable ingredients, such as plant-based oils, carnauba wax, and natural dyes. These products aim to provide the same level of care and shine without the negative environmental impact.

Technological advancements have also played a role in the modern evolution of shoe polish. The development of nano-technology, for instance, has led to the creation of water- and stain-resistant coatings that can be applied to shoes, offering long-lasting protection without the need for frequent polishing. These innovations reflect the ongoing effort to balance convenience, effectiveness, and environmental responsibility.

The cultural significance of shoe polish has evolved alongside its technological and chemical advancements. In many societies, polished shoes have been a symbol of attention to detail and personal pride. In the military, the ritual of polishing boots has been a part of discipline and uniformity. In professional settings, shiny shoes have often been associated with success and competence. This cultural dimension underscores the importance of shoe polish beyond its practical applications.

Furthermore, the rise of the fashion industry and the emphasis on personal style have influenced the demand for shoe polish. High-end leather goods and designer shoes require specialized care to maintain their appearance and value. This has led to the development of premium shoe care products and services, catering to discerning consumers who seek to preserve their investments in luxury footwear.

The global nature of modern commerce has also affected the shoe polish industry. Brands from different parts of the world compete in a diverse market, offering a wide range of products tailored to various preferences and needs. This international competition has spurred innovation and quality improvements, benefiting consumers with better choices and more effective solutions.

The evolution of shoe polish also includes a significant shift in how products are packaged and marketed. In the past, shoe polish was often sold in simple tins or bottles, with minimal branding. Today, packaging is an integral part of the product's appeal, with sleek designs, user-friendly applicators, and clear labeling that emphasizes benefits such as eco-friendliness or specific uses. This shift reflects broader trends in consumer goods, where aesthetics and branding play a crucial role in attracting and retaining customers.

Chapter 42: The Path of the Kitchen Sponge

The kitchen sponge, an essential item found in almost every household, has a history and evolution as intriguing as any other household object. Its path from natural origins to synthetic innovations reflects advancements in materials science, changes in consumer behavior, and the ongoing quest for hygiene and convenience in the kitchen. The journey of the kitchen sponge is intertwined with developments in chemistry, industrial manufacturing, and even ecological concerns, revealing a rich tapestry of history that extends far beyond its humble appearance.

The story of the kitchen sponge begins in ancient times, when people used natural materials for cleaning purposes. The earliest known sponges were natural sea sponges, harvested from the ocean. These sponges, belonging to the phylum Porifera, were prized for their absorbent properties and soft texture. Ancient Greeks and Romans were known to use natural sea sponges for bathing, cleaning, and even as tools for applying cosmetics and paints. The harvesting of sea sponges was a significant activity in coastal communities, where divers would collect them from the ocean floor.

Natural sea sponges remained the primary cleaning tool for centuries. They were used not only in households but also in various industries. For example, artists used sea sponges to apply and blend paints, while surgeons used them for medical purposes due to their softness and absorbency. The process of preparing natural sponges involved cleaning and bleaching them to remove any organic matter, leaving behind the porous skeleton that made them so effective at absorbing liquids.

The industrial revolution of the 19th century brought significant changes to the production and availability of cleaning tools, including sponges. The growth of urban centers and the development of new manufacturing techniques led to increased demand for affordable and efficient cleaning products. However, natural sea sponges had their limitations. They were relatively expensive, not always readily available, and their quality could vary depending on the source and harvesting methods.

The quest for a more consistent and affordable alternative to natural sponges led to the development of synthetic sponges. The invention of synthetic sponges can be traced back to the early 20th century, when advances in polymer chemistry allowed scientists to create new materials with properties similar to those of natural sponges. The first synthetic sponges were made from cellulose, a natural polymer derived from plant fibers such as wood pulp and cotton.

In 1927, the German company IG Farben developed a method to produce cellulose sponges on an industrial scale. The process involved dissolving cellulose in a chemical solution and then regenerating it into a sponge-like structure. This innovation marked a significant milestone in the history of cleaning products, as cellulose sponges were more affordable and readily available than their natural counterparts. They were also more uniform in quality and could be produced in large quantities to meet the growing demand.

The cellulose sponge quickly gained popularity due to its excellent absorbency, durability, and softness. It became a staple in households for cleaning dishes, countertops, and other surfaces. The success of cellulose sponges spurred further innovations in sponge technology, leading to the development of new materials and manufacturing techniques.

One of the most significant advancements in sponge technology came in the mid-20th century with the introduction of polyurethane foam. Polyurethane, a versatile synthetic polymer, offered several advantages over cellulose. It could be produced in a wide range of densities and textures, making it suitable for various cleaning applications. Polyurethane sponges were more resistant to wear and tear, had better scrubbing properties, and could be easily molded into different shapes and sizes.

The advent of polyurethane sponges coincided with the rise of consumer culture and the proliferation of household cleaning products. Manufacturers began producing sponges with different textures and features to cater to specific cleaning needs. For example, some sponges were designed with an abrasive surface on one side for scrubbing tough stains, while others had a softer side for gentle cleaning. The versatility of polyurethane foam allowed for endless possibilities in sponge design, making it a popular choice among consumers.

In addition to polyurethane, other synthetic materials such as polyester and nylon were also used to produce sponges. These materials offered unique properties that enhanced the functionality of sponges. Polyester sponges, for instance, were known for their resistance to mildew and odor, making them ideal for use in damp environments. Nylon sponges, on the other hand, were highly durable and could withstand repeated use without degrading.

The evolution of the kitchen sponge was not only driven by advancements in materials science but also by changing consumer preferences and concerns. In the latter half of the 20th century, there was growing awareness of hygiene and sanitation in the kitchen. This led to the development of sponges with antimicrobial properties, designed to inhibit the growth of bacteria and fungi. These sponges were treated with antimicrobial agents such as triclosan or silver nanoparticles, which helped to keep them cleaner and fresher for longer periods.

The introduction of antimicrobial sponges addressed concerns about the potential health risks associated with using sponges for cleaning. Studies had shown that kitchen sponges could harbor a significant number of bacteria, including harmful pathogens such as

E. coli and Salmonella. By incorporating antimicrobial agents into the sponge material, manufacturers aimed to reduce the risk of cross-contamination and improve overall kitchen hygiene.

However, the use of antimicrobial agents in sponges also raised environmental and health concerns. Some studies suggested that certain antimicrobial chemicals, such as triclosan, could have negative impacts on the environment and contribute to the development of antibiotic-resistant bacteria. These concerns led to increased scrutiny and regulatory actions, prompting manufacturers to explore alternative methods for enhancing sponge hygiene.

In recent years, the focus on sustainability and environmental responsibility has influenced the development of kitchen sponges. Consumers are increasingly seeking eco-friendly alternatives to traditional synthetic sponges, which are often made from non-biodegradable materials and can contribute to plastic pollution. In response, manufacturers have introduced a variety of biodegradable and compostable sponges made from natural fibers such as cellulose, coconut coir, and bamboo.

These eco-friendly sponges offer a more sustainable option for consumers who are concerned about the environmental impact of their cleaning products. Biodegradable sponges break down naturally over time, reducing the amount of waste that ends up in landfills. Some companies have also developed sponges made from recycled materials, further minimizing their environmental footprint.

The rise of the green movement has also led to increased interest in DIY and zero-waste alternatives to conventional sponges. Many people are turning to natural materials such as loofahs, plant-based cloths, and even homemade sponges made from knitted or crocheted yarn. These alternatives reflect a growing desire to reduce reliance on single-use plastics and embrace more sustainable cleaning practices.

Chapter 43: The Creation of the Dustpan and Brush

The creation and evolution of the dustpan and brush are integral to understanding the history of household cleaning tools. These seemingly simple items have undergone significant transformations in design, materials, and functionality over centuries. They have mirrored societal changes, advancements in technology, and shifts in domestic responsibilities. The story of the dustpan and brush is one of ingenuity, adaptation, and cultural significance.

The origins of the dustpan and brush can be traced back to ancient times when people first began to develop tools to aid in cleaning. Early methods for sweeping floors involved using simple bundles of twigs or reeds, which were effective but not particularly efficient. These primitive brushes were used to sweep debris into a designated area, often collected by hand or with the aid of a flat object. These flat objects, which can be considered early forms of dustpans, were likely made from materials readily available in nature, such as large leaves, pieces of bark, or flat stones.

As civilizations advanced, so did their tools for cleaning. In ancient Egypt, brushes were made from palm fronds and other plant materials bound together. These early brushes were used not only for sweeping floors but also for applying cleaning agents to surfaces. The Egyptians were known for their emphasis on cleanliness and hygiene, and their innovations in cleaning tools reflect this cultural value. The concept of using a separate tool to collect swept debris began to take shape during this period, though it would still be many centuries before the modern dustpan emerged.

The Romans, renowned for their engineering and domestic innovations, further refined cleaning tools. They developed brooms made from twigs and other plant materials, which were more effective at sweeping debris. However, the process of collecting the debris was still rudimentary, involving scooping it up by hand or using flat objects. The Romans' contributions to public sanitation and urban living created a demand for more effective cleaning methods, setting the stage for future advancements.

The Middle Ages saw limited progress in the development of cleaning tools. Household cleaning was largely the responsibility of servants in wealthy households or family members in poorer ones. Brooms and brushes continued to be made from natural materials, and the practice of collecting debris by hand persisted. However, this period laid the groundwork for future innovations by maintaining the cultural importance of cleanliness and domestic order.

The Renaissance brought about significant advancements in many areas, including the arts, science, and domestic life. The increased availability of materials and the rise of skilled craftsmen led to the creation of more refined and effective cleaning tools. Brushes made from animal hair or bristles became more common, offering improved durability and effectiveness. The concept of a dedicated tool for collecting debris, resembling a dustpan, began to emerge more clearly during this period.

The 18th and 19th centuries marked a turning point in the history of the dustpan and brush, driven by the Industrial Revolution and the rise of mass production. The development of new materials and manufacturing techniques allowed for the creation of more sophisticated and affordable cleaning tools. One of the most significant innovations during this period was the introduction of metal dustpans. These early metal dustpans were typically made from tin or iron and featured a flat surface with raised edges to contain debris. They were a marked improvement over previous methods, allowing for more efficient and hygienic collection of swept material.

In 1858, American inventor T.E. McNeill patented the first dustpan with a handle, revolutionizing its design and usability. This innovation made it possible to collect debris without bending down, greatly improving comfort and efficiency. McNeill's design featured a flat metal pan with a long wooden handle, a configuration that remains common in dustpans to this day. This invention was quickly adopted in households and commercial settings, underscoring the demand for more ergonomic cleaning tools.

The development of synthetic materials in the late 19th and early 20th centuries further transformed the dustpan and brush. The invention of plastics allowed for the creation of lightweight, durable, and cost-effective cleaning tools. Plastic dustpans became widely available, offering advantages over metal versions, such as resistance to rust and ease of manufacturing. Brushes also saw significant improvements, with synthetic bristles replacing natural materials. These synthetic bristles were more durable, resistant to moisture, and could be produced in various stiffness levels to suit different cleaning tasks.

The mid-20th century saw continued innovation in the design and functionality of the dustpan and brush. Manufacturers began to focus on creating more user-friendly products, incorporating features such as rubber edges on dustpans to improve debris collection and reduce scratching on floors. Ergonomic handles became more common, designed to reduce strain on the user's wrist and back. These improvements reflected a growing awareness of the importance of ergonomics and user comfort in household tools.

The cultural significance of the dustpan and brush also evolved during this period. As domestic responsibilities became more evenly distributed between men and women, and as the rise of consumer culture emphasized convenience and efficiency, the demand for effective cleaning tools increased. The dustpan and brush became symbols of modern domesticity, reflecting broader societal changes in the perception of household chores and cleanliness.

The late 20th and early 21st centuries have seen a continued focus on innovation and sustainability in the design of the dustpan and brush. As environmental concerns have grown, manufacturers have explored the use of eco-friendly materials, such as recycled plastics and biodegradable components. This shift reflects a broader trend towards sustainability in consumer products, driven by increased awareness of the environmental impact of household items.

Technological advancements have also played a role in the evolution of the dustpan and brush. The integration of modern manufacturing techniques, such as injection molding and advanced polymer science, has allowed for the creation of more precise and durable products. Some dustpans now feature built-in combs or teeth for cleaning the brush bristles, enhancing their functionality and convenience.

The rise of digital technology has also influenced the marketing and distribution of dustpans and brushes. Online retail platforms have made it easier for consumers to access a wide range of cleaning tools, compare features, and read reviews. This increased access to information has empowered consumers to make more informed choices, driving demand for high-quality, innovative products.

In addition to practical improvements, the design of dustpans and brushes has also been influenced by aesthetics. Manufacturers recognize that consumers increasingly view household tools as an extension of their personal style and home decor. As a result, there has been a trend towards more visually appealing designs, with dustpans and brushes available in a variety of colors, shapes, and finishes. This focus on aesthetics reflects a broader cultural shift towards the integration of form and function in everyday objects.

The evolution of the dustpan and brush is also a story of globalization. As manufacturing and trade networks have expanded, cleaning tools have become more widely available and affordable. Innovations and design trends from different parts of the world have influenced each other, leading to a rich diversity of products that cater to various cultural preferences and cleaning practices.

Chapter 44: The Advent of the Contact Lens

The advent of the contact lens is a fascinating story that spans centuries, encompassing a range of scientific disciplines, technological advancements, and evolving consumer needs. The journey from conceptualization to modern-day contact lenses involved pioneering efforts by visionaries, advancements in material science, and an ongoing quest to improve visual acuity and comfort. Understanding the history of contact lenses offers insights into the broader context of medical innovation and the continuous drive to enhance quality of life.

The concept of contact lenses dates back to the Renaissance, a period of immense intellectual and scientific progress. Leonardo da Vinci is often credited with the first known exploration of the concept of contact lenses. In his 1508 manuscript, the Codex of the Eye, da Vinci illustrated and described a method for altering vision by submerging the eye in a bowl of water. While this was not a practical solution, it laid the groundwork for the idea that vision could be corrected through direct contact with the eye.

The next significant contribution came from the 17th-century philosopher and scientist René Descartes. In 1636, Descartes proposed a device consisting of a glass tube filled with liquid and placed directly on the cornea. While this design was also impractical due to the tube's length preventing blinking, it demonstrated an early understanding of refractive correction through contact with the eye's surface.

The 19th century saw the first practical attempts to create contact lenses. German glassblower F. A. Muller is credited with creating the first known glass contact lens in 1887. This lens was designed to cover the entire eye and was used primarily for therapeutic purposes rather than vision correction. However, these early glass lenses were heavy, uncomfortable, and could only be worn for short periods due to the lack of oxygen permeability, leading to significant discomfort and potential damage to the eye.

It was not until the late 19th and early 20th centuries that significant advancements were made in contact lens technology. Adolf Fick, a Swiss physician, and Eugene Kalt, a French optometrist, independently developed the first successful glass contact lenses for vision correction in the late 1880s. These lenses were still large and uncomfortable but represented a crucial step forward in the development of contact lenses.

The early 20th century saw further advancements in materials and design. In the 1930s, German optometrist William Feinbloom introduced plastic lenses, which were lighter and more comfortable than their glass predecessors. Feinbloom's lenses combined glass and plastic, reducing the weight and improving comfort, but they still covered the entire sclera, the white part of the eye, limiting their practicality for extended wear.

A major breakthrough came in the 1940s with the development of corneal lenses, which covered only the cornea rather than the entire eye. Hungarian ophthalmologist Dr. István Györffy and optometrist Kevin Tuohy independently developed these smaller, more comfortable lenses. Tuohy's lenses were made entirely of plastic, specifically polymethyl methacrylate (PMMA), which allowed for better oxygen permeability and increased comfort. These lenses marked a significant shift toward modern contact lenses, as they could be worn for longer periods without causing as much discomfort or eye irritation.

The next major milestone in the evolution of contact lenses was the development of soft lenses. In the 1960s, Czech chemist Otto Wichterle and his assistant Drahoslav Lím invented hydrogel, a water-absorbing plastic material that led to the creation of the first soft contact lenses. These lenses, made from a material called polyhydroxyethylmethacrylate (HEMA), were far more comfortable than rigid lenses, as they allowed oxygen to pass through to the cornea and conformed to the shape of the eye.

Wichterle's innovation revolutionized the contact lens industry. Soft lenses provided unprecedented comfort and could be worn for extended periods, making them suitable for daily use. This development also opened the door for disposable lenses, which would become a significant market segment in later years. The commercialization of soft lenses began in the early 1970s, with Bausch & Lomb becoming one of the first companies to market them successfully.

The 1980s and 1990s saw rapid advancements in contact lens technology, driven by improvements in materials and manufacturing processes. The introduction of silicone hydrogel lenses in the late 1990s represented a significant leap forward. Silicone hydrogel lenses allowed even greater oxygen permeability than traditional hydrogel lenses, reducing the risk of complications such as corneal hypoxia. These lenses could be worn continuously for extended periods, including overnight, without compromising eye health.

The advent of disposable contact lenses further transformed the market. In the late 1980s, Johnson & Johnson's Acuvue brand introduced the first disposable lenses, designed to be worn for a short period and then discarded. This innovation addressed concerns about lens hygiene and maintenance, reducing the risk of eye infections and making contact lens wear more convenient for users. Daily disposable lenses, introduced in the 1990s, took this concept a step further by eliminating the need for cleaning solutions and storage cases altogether.

Technological advancements also led to the development of specialized contact lenses for various vision correction needs. Toric lenses were designed to correct astigmatism, while multifocal lenses provided solutions for presbyopia, allowing users to see clearly at multiple distances. Advances in lens design and manufacturing techniques, such as aspheric lenses and wavefront technology, improved visual acuity and comfort for contact lens wearers.

In addition to vision correction, contact lenses began to be used for cosmetic purposes. Colored and decorative lenses allowed users to change their eye color or create dramatic effects for special occasions. These lenses gained popularity not only for personal use but also in the entertainment industry, where they were used to create striking visual effects in movies and theater productions.

The digital age brought new challenges and opportunities for the contact lens industry. The increasing prevalence of digital screens led to a rise in conditions such as digital eye strain and dry eye syndrome. In response, manufacturers developed lenses with enhanced moisture retention and blue light filtering capabilities to address these issues. The integration of smart technology into contact lenses also emerged as a frontier for innovation. Researchers began exploring the potential for lenses that could monitor health metrics, deliver medications, or even provide augmented reality displays.

The history of contact lenses is also marked by significant advancements in the understanding of ocular physiology and the impact of lenses on eye health. Early contact lenses posed risks such as corneal abrasion, hypoxia, and infections due to poor oxygen permeability and hygiene practices. Advances in materials and design have significantly mitigated these risks, but ongoing research continues to improve the safety and efficacy of contact lenses.

The regulatory landscape for contact lenses has evolved alongside technological advancements. In the United States, the Food and Drug Administration (FDA) plays a crucial role in ensuring the safety and effectiveness of contact lenses. The FDA's classification system and rigorous approval process have helped maintain high standards in the industry. Internationally, various regulatory bodies have implemented similar standards to protect consumers and promote the safe use of contact lenses.

The evolution of contact lenses has also been influenced by broader trends in healthcare and consumer behavior. The shift towards preventive care and personalized medicine has driven demand for contact lenses that address specific vision needs and provide added health benefits. The rise of e-commerce has transformed the way consumers purchase contact lenses, with online retailers offering convenience and competitive pricing. Telemedicine has also impacted the industry, enabling remote eye exams and prescription renewals, making contact lens access more convenient for users.

Sustainability has become an increasingly important consideration in the contact lens industry. The environmental impact of disposable lenses and their packaging has prompted manufacturers to explore eco-friendly alternatives. Efforts to reduce plastic waste include the development of biodegradable materials, recycling programs for used lenses and packaging, and initiatives to raise awareness about proper disposal practices.

Chapter 45: The Origin of the Sticky Note

The sticky note, a ubiquitous office supply today, has a history rooted in a combination of accidental discovery and innovative thinking. Its origin dates back to the late 1960s and early 1970s, when 3M, a company renowned for its inventive solutions, became the birthplace of this simple yet revolutionary product. The journey of the sticky note began with a failed experiment by Dr. Spencer Silver, a chemist at 3M, who was working on developing a strong adhesive for the aerospace industry. In 1968, Silver stumbled upon an adhesive that was not strong at all; instead, it was a low-tack, pressure-sensitive adhesive that adhered lightly to surfaces but could be easily removed without leaving residue.

Although Silver recognized the potential of his discovery, he struggled to find a practical application for it. He tirelessly promoted the unique adhesive within 3M, conducting seminars and presentations to spark interest among his colleagues. Despite his enthusiasm, finding a use for an adhesive that didn't adhere permanently proved challenging. The breakthrough came several years later, thanks to Art Fry, a fellow 3M scientist and a church choir member. Fry was frustrated with the paper bookmarks he used in his hymnal, which frequently slipped out and lost his place. Remembering Silver's adhesive, Fry had an epiphany: a bookmark that could stick to the paper without damaging it would be the perfect solution. He envisioned small pieces of paper coated with the adhesive that could be easily applied and removed.

In 1974, Fry began experimenting with Silver's adhesive, applying it to small pieces of paper. He tested his prototype bookmarks in his hymnal and found they worked perfectly, staying in place and easily repositionable. Excited by the potential, Fry continued refining his idea, eventually creating the first version of what would become the sticky note. He shared his invention with colleagues, who quickly saw its practicality in everyday office use, such as leaving notes and reminders.

3M decided to market the product, initially naming it "Press 'n Peel" in 1977 and conducting test markets in select cities. The response was lukewarm; consumers didn't immediately grasp the product's versatility. Undeterred, 3M rebranded the product as "Post-it Notes" and launched an extensive marketing campaign. This time, the response was overwhelmingly positive. People quickly recognized the convenience and utility of sticky notes for note-taking, reminders, and organization. By 1980, Post-it Notes were being sold nationwide in the United States, and their popularity soon spread globally.

The success of sticky notes can be attributed to their simplicity and adaptability. They provided a practical solution to everyday problems, from marking pages in books to leaving messages for colleagues. The adhesive's unique properties, allowing it to stick and be repositioned without damage, made sticky notes a versatile tool in various settings, including offices, schools, and homes. Over the years, the product has evolved, with 3M introducing different sizes, shapes, and colors to cater to diverse needs. The original canary yellow color was chosen because it was the only scrap paper available at the time, but it became iconic. Today, sticky notes come in a rainbow of colors, adding a touch of personalization and fun to their practical use.

In addition to the classic square notes, 3M has developed a range of related products, such as lined sticky notes for more organized writing, larger pads for more detailed messages, and even digital versions integrated into computer software and mobile apps. The sticky note's impact on workplace efficiency and personal organization cannot be overstated. It revolutionized how people manage tasks, collaborate, and communicate, offering a simple yet effective method to keep track of information and ideas. The adhesive's gentle tackiness ensured that notes could be moved and removed without damage, a feature that set them apart from other types of adhesive paper products.

Moreover, sticky notes have transcended their original purpose, becoming a medium for creativity and expression. People use them for brainstorming sessions, creating art installations, and even leaving positive messages in public spaces. The sticky note's versatility has made it a cultural icon, symbolizing innovation born from an unexpected discovery. The story of the sticky note also highlights the importance of perseverance and cross-disciplinary collaboration in innovation. Dr. Spencer Silver's adhesive might have remained an unused curiosity without Art Fry's inventive application. Their combined efforts, supported by 3M's commitment to nurturing new ideas, turned a serendipitous discovery into a globally recognized and indispensable product.

In educational settings, sticky notes have become a staple for both teachers and students. They are used for everything from annotating reading materials to organizing study notes and creating interactive learning experiences. The ability to easily move notes around fosters a dynamic and engaging approach to learning, encouraging students to actively participate and collaborate. The sticky note's journey from a failed adhesive to a ubiquitous office supply is a testament to the power of innovation and the unexpected paths it can take. It underscores the value of embracing failure as a step toward success and the importance of keeping an open mind to new possibilities. Dr. Silver's and Art Fry's story serves as an inspiration for inventors and innovators everywhere, reminding us that sometimes the most significant breakthroughs come from the most unexpected places.

The enduring popularity of sticky notes also reflects their adaptability to changing times and needs. In an increasingly digital world, where communication often happens through screens, the tactile and visual nature of sticky notes offers a refreshing and effective complement to digital tools. They provide a physical presence that can enhance memory and organization, bridging the gap between the digital and physical worlds.

Chapter 46: The Tale of the Sewing Needle

The sewing needle, a seemingly simple yet indispensable tool, has a rich and intricate history that stretches back thousands of years. Its development mirrors the progress of human civilization, reflecting advancements in technology, culture, and society. The tale of the sewing needle begins in prehistoric times, with the earliest known needles dating back to around 50,000 years ago. These primitive needles were made from bone and ivory, meticulously crafted by our ancestors to stitch together animal hides and other materials for clothing and shelter. These early tools were crucial for survival, enabling early humans to create more effective and protective garments suited to various climates.

As human societies evolved, so did the technology of needle-making. During the Upper Paleolithic period, around 30,000 years ago, more sophisticated bone needles with eyelets were developed, allowing for the use of thread. These advancements coincided with the domestication of animals like sheep and goats, which provided wool and other fibers that could be spun into thread. The combination of new materials and improved tools marked significant progress in the creation of clothing, fostering greater specialization and craftsmanship.

The invention of metallurgy around 5,000 years ago revolutionized needle-making. Bronze and later iron needles became common, offering greater durability and precision. Ancient civilizations such as the Egyptians, Greeks, and Romans utilized metal needles, which facilitated more intricate and refined sewing techniques. In Egypt, needles made from copper and bronze have been discovered in tombs, indicating their importance in both daily life and burial practices. These needles were used not only for sewing garments but also for intricate embroidery, showcasing the early development of decorative arts.

The spread of needle-making knowledge and techniques was significantly influenced by trade and cultural exchanges. The Silk Road, a vast network of trade routes connecting the East and West, played a crucial role in disseminating needle technology across continents. Chinese innovations, such as the use of fine silk threads and the development of steel needles, had a profound impact on needle production and textile arts in regions as far away as Europe. By the medieval period, needle-making had become a specialized craft in many cultures. In Europe, guilds were established to regulate and protect the trade of needle-making. These guilds ensured high standards of quality and craftsmanship, as needles were essential tools for tailors, cobblers, and other artisans. During this time, steel needles became the norm, valued for their strength and sharpness. The production of needles involved complex processes, including drawing steel wire, hardening, and tempering, followed by the meticulous creation of the eyelet and point.

The Renaissance period saw further advancements in needle production and the expansion of textile arts. The increased availability of high-quality needles contributed to the flourishing of embroidery, lace-making, and other intricate sewing techniques. In the 16th century, the city of Nuremberg in Germany emerged as a major center for needle manufacturing, producing some of the finest needles in Europe. The Nuremberg needles were renowned for their exceptional quality and were exported widely, influencing sewing practices across the continent.

The Industrial Revolution in the 18th and 19th centuries marked a turning point in the history of the sewing needle. The advent of machinery enabled the mass production of needles, making them more affordable and accessible. Factories employed specialized machines to draw, cut, and shape steel wire into needles, significantly increasing production efficiency. One of the notable inventions during this period was the sewing machine, patented by Elias Howe in 1846. The sewing machine revolutionized the textile industry, transforming the way clothing and textiles were produced. While the sewing machine did not render hand sewing obsolete, it complemented traditional techniques and increased productivity. The invention of machine needles, specifically designed for use in sewing machines, further diversified the types of needles available.

In the late 19th and early 20th centuries, needle production became a global industry, with significant centers in England, Germany, and the United States. The town of Redditch in England became particularly famous for its needle production, earning the moniker "The Needle Capital of the World." Redditch needles were celebrated for their precision and quality, a testament to the town's skilled workforce and advanced manufacturing techniques.

The 20th century saw continued innovation in needle design and materials. Stainless steel and other alloys were introduced, enhancing the durability and resistance to corrosion. New types of needles were developed to meet the specific needs of different sewing techniques and fabrics. For example, ballpoint needles were created for use with knit fabrics, reducing the risk of damaging the material. The rise of synthetic fibers and the development of new fabrics also influenced needle design, leading to the creation of specialized needles for materials such as nylon and polyester.

Beyond their practical applications, sewing needles have also played a significant role in cultural and artistic expression. Needlework, including embroidery, quilting, and tapestry, has been a means of storytelling, cultural preservation, and artistic expression across various cultures. Traditional needlework techniques and patterns have been passed down through generations, preserving the heritage and identity of communities.

In contemporary times, the humble sewing needle continues to be an essential tool in both professional and domestic settings. While advanced machinery and technology have transformed the textile and garment industries, hand sewing remains a vital skill, cherished for its precision and personal touch. Hobbyists and artisans around the world use needles to create handmade garments, accessories, and works of art, celebrating the timeless craft of sewing.

Moreover, the needle has found applications beyond textiles, in fields such as medicine and technology. Surgical needles, for instance, are critical tools in medical procedures, enabling precise suturing and wound closure. The development of minimally invasive surgical techniques has further expanded the use of specialized needles in medical practice. In the realm of technology, needles are used in various precision instruments and devices, underscoring their versatility and enduring relevance.

Chapter 47: The Rise of the USB Drive

The USB drive, or Universal Serial Bus drive, also known as a flash drive, thumb drive, or pen drive, has become an indispensable tool for data storage and transfer in the digital age. Its rise to prominence is a story of technological innovation, market demand, and the evolution of data management practices. This journey begins in the late 20th century and encompasses a series of developments that revolutionized how we store, share, and transport digital information.

Before the advent of the USB drive, data storage and transfer relied heavily on earlier technologies such as floppy disks, CDs, and DVDs. Floppy disks, introduced in the 1970s, were among the first portable storage devices, allowing users to store small amounts of data—initially a few kilobytes, later expanding to 1.44 megabytes in the most popular 3.5-inch format. However, their limited storage capacity and susceptibility to damage posed significant limitations. CDs and DVDs, emerging in the 1980s and 1990s, offered a substantial increase in storage capacity, with CDs holding up to 700 megabytes and DVDs up to 4.7 gigabytes. Despite this improvement, they were still relatively slow to write to, not very portable, and required specific hardware to read and write data.

The development of the USB drive was driven by the need for a more reliable, higher-capacity, and portable storage solution. The roots of USB technology trace back to the mid-1990s when several major technology companies, including Intel, Microsoft, IBM, and Compaq, collaborated to create a standardized interface for connecting peripherals to computers. The goal was to replace the multitude of connectors at the back of PCs and simplify the process of adding new devices. This led to the creation of the USB standard, which was first released in 1996.

The first USB flash drive was developed in the late 1990s. Israeli company M-Systems, co-founded by Dov Moran, is often credited with creating the first commercially available USB flash drive. Their product, called the DiskOnKey, was released in 2000 and offered a storage capacity of 8 megabytes—small by today's standards but a significant advancement at the time. The DiskOnKey was revolutionary because it combined flash memory technology with the USB interface, providing a durable, rewritable, and highly portable storage solution.

The rise of the USB drive can be attributed to several key factors. Firstly, the use of flash memory was a major breakthrough. Flash memory, a type of non-volatile storage that retains data without power, was more durable and reliable than the magnetic storage used in floppy disks and the optical storage used in CDs and DVDs. Flash memory's compact size also enabled the creation of smaller, more portable devices.

Secondly, the USB interface itself was instrumental in the success of the USB drive. The USB port, becoming a standard feature on computers and laptops, provided a universal connection method that was easy to use. Users could plug in a USB drive and have it recognized by the computer almost instantly, without the need for additional drivers or complex setup procedures. This plug-and-play capability greatly enhanced the usability and convenience of USB drives.

Thirdly, rapid advancements in flash memory technology allowed for significant increases in storage capacity and reductions in cost. Early USB drives, like the DiskOnKey, started with modest capacities, but within a few years, drives with capacities of hundreds of megabytes and then several gigabytes became available. This exponential growth in storage capacity, coupled with declining prices, made USB drives an attractive option for both personal and professional use.

As USB drives gained popularity, they began to displace older storage media. Their advantages over floppy disks, CDs, and DVDs were clear: greater storage capacity, faster data transfer speeds, and superior durability. USB drives were less susceptible to physical damage, such as scratches or magnetic interference, and could be easily carried in a pocket or attached to a keychain. These features made them ideal for a wide range of applications, from transferring files between computers to backing up important data.

The early 2000s saw a proliferation of USB drive manufacturers, with companies like SanDisk, Kingston, and Lexar entering the market. Competition drove further innovation and price reductions, making USB drives accessible to a broader audience. The design of USB drives also evolved, with manufacturers experimenting with different form factors, materials, and additional features such as encryption and password protection.

USB drives also found applications beyond simple data storage. They became popular as promotional items, with companies branding drives with their logos and preloading them with marketing materials. Some USB drives were designed with specialized functions, such as bootable drives for installing operating systems or drives with built-in security features for safeguarding sensitive information.

The mid-2000s marked another significant development in the rise of USB drives: the introduction of USB 2.0. Released in 2000, USB 2.0 offered a significant increase in data transfer speeds, up to 480 megabits per second, compared to the original USB 1.1 standard's 12 megabits per second. This improvement made USB drives even more efficient for transferring large files, such as high-resolution images, videos, and software applications.

The introduction of USB 3.0 in 2008 further propelled the capabilities of USB drives. USB 3.0 offered data transfer speeds up to 5 gigabits per second, significantly reducing the time required to transfer large amounts of data. This new standard was backward compatible with USB 2.0, ensuring that users could continue to use their existing devices while benefiting from the enhanced performance of USB 3.0 drives. Subsequent iterations, such as USB 3.1 and USB 3.2, have continued to push the boundaries of speed and efficiency, with USB 3.2 offering speeds up to 20 gigabits per second.

In addition to speed improvements, the rise of USB-C, introduced in 2014, brought further advancements in the versatility and usability of USB drives. USB-C, with its reversible connector, eliminated the frustration of aligning the plug correctly, making it even more user-friendly. USB-C also supported higher power delivery, enabling faster charging and the ability to power larger devices, further expanding the utility of USB drives.

Despite the advent of cloud storage solutions, which offer the convenience of accessing data from anywhere with an internet connection, USB drives have retained their relevance. They provide a reliable, offline method of data storage and transfer, crucial in scenarios where internet access is limited or security concerns dictate the need for physical data transfer. USB drives also offer advantages in terms of speed and ease of use, particularly for large files or sensitive data that users prefer not to upload to the cloud.

The versatility of USB drives continues to grow as they are integrated into various devices and applications. From bootable drives used in IT maintenance and recovery operations to portable media libraries for photographers and videographers, USB drives have become essential tools in numerous fields. Their small size and high capacity make them ideal for use in embedded systems, automotive applications, and portable entertainment systems.

In recent years, advancements in security features have made USB drives even more appealing for professional and enterprise use. Hardware encryption, biometric authentication, and secure access controls have been incorporated into USB drives to protect sensitive data from unauthorized access. These features have made USB drives a trusted solution for industries that require stringent data security measures, such as healthcare, finance, and government.

The environmental impact of USB drives has also come under consideration, with manufacturers exploring ways to make them more sustainable. Efforts include using recycled materials, reducing packaging waste, and developing more energy-efficient production processes. As technology continues to evolve, the future of USB drives will likely see further enhancements in capacity, speed, and security, while also addressing environmental concerns.

Chapter 48: The Discovery of the Ice Cube Tray

The discovery and evolution of the ice cube tray is a fascinating journey that intertwines with the history of refrigeration, food preservation, and even social customs. Ice, in its simplest form, has long been valued for its cooling properties, but the ability to produce and store ice cubes in individual, manageable portions is a relatively modern innovation. The ice cube tray, an essential household item today, has its origins rooted in the late 19th and early 20th centuries, a period marked by significant advancements in refrigeration technology and domestic conveniences.

Before the advent of mechanical refrigeration, people relied on natural ice harvested from lakes and rivers during winter. This ice was stored in ice houses, insulated structures designed to keep ice frozen for use in the warmer months. Ice was a luxury item, primarily enjoyed by the wealthy for cooling drinks and preserving food. The ice trade, which developed in the 19th century, involved the large-scale harvesting and transportation of natural ice, creating a burgeoning industry that spanned continents. However, the reliance on natural ice was fraught with challenges, including variability in ice quality, contamination, and the logistical difficulties of storage and transport.

The development of mechanical refrigeration systems in the late 19th century revolutionized the production and storage of ice. Early refrigeration technologies were primarily used for industrial applications, such as meatpacking and brewing, where the need for consistent and reliable cooling was critical. These early systems were bulky, expensive, and not suitable for domestic use. However, as technology progressed, smaller, more efficient refrigeration units began to be developed for home use.

One of the earliest known ice cube trays dates back to 1844, attributed to John Gorrie, an American physician and inventor. Gorrie designed an ice-making machine to produce artificial ice, intended to cool the air for patients suffering from yellow fever and other illnesses. His invention laid the groundwork for mechanical refrigeration, although it did not lead directly to the creation of the modern ice cube tray. Gorrie's pioneering work demonstrated the potential for artificial ice production and the health benefits of a cool environment, influencing future innovations in refrigeration.

The first patent for an ice cube tray was granted to Guy L. Tinkham in 1933. Tinkham, who worked for the General Utilities Manufacturing Company, developed a simple yet effective design: a metal tray with a grid of dividers, which could be filled with water and frozen to produce uniform ice cubes. This design allowed for easy removal of the cubes by twisting or flexing the tray. Tinkham's invention was a significant improvement over previous methods, which often involved chipping ice from larger blocks, a labor-intensive and imprecise process.

The introduction of Tinkham's ice cube tray coincided with the increasing availability of domestic refrigerators, making it possible for households to produce and store ice conveniently. These early trays were typically made of metal, which conducted heat efficiently, allowing the ice to freeze quickly and release easily from the tray. The convenience and practicality of the ice cube tray quickly made it a popular household item, transforming the way people used and consumed ice.

During the mid-20th century, the design and materials of ice cube trays continued to evolve. The advent of plastic materials, particularly polyethylene and polypropylene, revolutionized the production of ice cube trays. Plastic trays were lighter, more flexible, and less prone to corrosion compared to metal trays. They also allowed for more intricate and varied designs, including trays with different shapes and sizes of compartments. The flexibility of plastic made it easier to remove ice cubes by simply twisting or bending the tray, a significant improvement in user convenience.

One notable innovation in ice cube tray design was the development of the "crack-and-twist" tray by Lloyd Groff Copeman, an American inventor, in the 1930s. Copeman's tray featured a series of individual cells connected by thin walls. When the tray was twisted, the thin walls would crack, and the ice cubes would be released. This design simplified the process of ice cube removal and became the basis for many subsequent designs.

Another significant advancement was the introduction of the lever-release tray in the 1950s. This design, often attributed to inventor Frank W. Farrell, incorporated a lever mechanism that could be lifted to release the ice cubes from the tray. The lever-release tray provided a mechanical advantage, making it easier to remove ice cubes without excessive twisting or bending. This design gained widespread popularity and remains in use today in various forms.

As household freezers became more commonplace in the post-World War II era, the demand for convenient ice-making solutions grew. Ice cube trays became a standard feature in refrigerators, and manufacturers continued to refine and improve their designs. The development of automatic ice makers in the 1960s further transformed the landscape of domestic ice production. These built-in appliances could produce ice continuously, eliminating the need for manual filling and emptying of trays. While automatic ice makers offered unparalleled convenience, ice cube trays remained a staple for those without such features or for those needing additional ice.

The cultural significance of ice and ice cube trays also evolved over time. In the mid-20th century, the availability of ice became associated with modernity and convenience. Ice cubes were no longer a luxury but an expectation in households across the socioeconomic spectrum. The ability to serve cold drinks, preserve food, and create ice-based treats became an integral part of domestic life. Ice cube trays played a crucial role in this cultural shift, democratizing access to ice and enhancing everyday living.

In addition to their practical uses, ice cube trays found creative and unconventional applications. The versatility of plastic allowed for the creation of trays in various shapes and sizes, catering to a range of uses beyond simply cooling drinks. Novelty ice cube trays, designed to produce ice cubes in fun shapes like stars, hearts, and animals, became popular for parties and special occasions. Ice cube trays were also used for freezing portions of food, such as herbs, baby food, and stock, providing a convenient way to store and preserve small quantities.

The environmental impact of disposable ice packs and the increasing interest in sustainability have also influenced the design and use of ice cube trays. Reusable ice cubes, made from materials like stainless steel or silicone, offer an eco-friendly alternative to traditional ice cubes. These reusable options can be chilled in the freezer and used repeatedly, reducing the need for single-use plastic ice packs.

In recent years, technological advancements have continued to shape the evolution of ice cube trays. Innovations such as silicone trays with flexible bottoms, which allow for easy popping out of individual ice cubes, have enhanced user convenience. Additionally, the integration of advanced materials like silicone and BPA-free plastics has addressed health and safety concerns, ensuring that ice cube trays are safe for food use.

Chapter 49: The Story of the Ball Bearing

The story of the ball bearing is one of ingenuity, mechanical innovation, and the relentless pursuit of efficiency and precision. Ball bearings are ubiquitous in modern machinery, from simple household appliances to complex industrial equipment and vehicles, playing a crucial role in reducing friction and enabling smooth rotational motion. Their development is deeply intertwined with the history of engineering and manufacturing, reflecting broader technological advancements and societal needs.

The concept of reducing friction dates back to ancient times. Early humans recognized the benefits of rolling objects rather than dragging them. Evidence suggests that the ancient Egyptians used cylindrical rollers to move massive stone blocks, a primitive form of the bearing principle. Similarly, the Greeks and Romans employed rotating mechanisms, such as wheels and axles, to facilitate movement and reduce friction in various applications.

The first documented use of bearings can be traced to the Roman Empire. The remains of wooden bearings were discovered in Roman ships and chariots, indicating an early understanding of the benefits of reducing friction through rolling elements. However, these early bearings were rudimentary and lacked the precision and durability of modern designs.

The Renaissance period marked a significant advancement in the understanding and application of bearing principles. Leonardo da Vinci, the quintessential Renaissance polymath, made detailed sketches and studies of various mechanical devices, including early concepts of ball bearings. In his notebooks, da Vinci illustrated a design for a ball bearing that used a series of balls to reduce friction between two rotating surfaces. While his designs were never built during his lifetime, they demonstrated a profound understanding of the mechanics of rolling elements and their potential applications.

The Industrial Revolution in the 18th and 19th centuries was a pivotal period for the development of ball bearings. The rapid growth of industry and manufacturing created a pressing need for more efficient and reliable machinery. Traditional methods of reducing friction, such as lubricants and plain bearings, were insufficient for the demands of new industrial applications. This period saw significant advancements in materials science, machining, and engineering, laying the groundwork for the modern ball bearing.

One of the earliest patents for a ball bearing was granted to Philip Vaughan, a Welsh inventor, in 1794. Vaughan's design featured a ball bearing housed in a carriage axle, allowing the wheels to rotate more smoothly and with less friction. This invention represented a significant improvement over previous designs, providing a practical solution for reducing friction in wheeled vehicles. Vaughan's ball bearing design was a precursor to modern bearing technology, incorporating many principles that are still used today.

The 19th century saw further innovations in ball bearing design and manufacturing. The advent of precision machining techniques enabled the production of more accurate and consistent bearing components. Henry Timken, an American inventor and businessman, patented the tapered roller bearing in 1898, which used conical rollers instead of balls to handle both radial and axial loads more effectively. Timken's invention was particularly well-suited for applications involving heavy loads and high speeds, such as in railway cars and industrial machinery.

The early 20th century marked the beginning of the modern era of ball bearings. Sven Wingquist, a Swedish engineer, made a groundbreaking contribution with his invention of the self-aligning ball bearing in 1907. Wingquist's design featured a double-row of balls and a spherical outer raceway, allowing the bearing to accommodate misalignment and shaft deflection. This innovation greatly improved the reliability and performance of ball bearings in various applications, from automotive to industrial machinery. Wingquist founded the Svenska Kullagerfabriken (SKF), which became one of the world's leading bearing manufacturers, driving further advancements in bearing technology and production.

During the 20th century, the development of new materials and manufacturing techniques further enhanced the performance and durability of ball bearings. The use of high-quality steel alloys and advanced heat treatment processes improved the strength and wear resistance of bearing components. The introduction of synthetic lubricants and seals extended the lifespan of bearings and reduced maintenance requirements. These advancements made ball bearings more reliable and capable of handling higher loads and speeds.

World War II played a significant role in accelerating the development and production of ball bearings. The demand for high-performance bearings for military vehicles, aircraft, and industrial machinery drove innovation and investment in bearing technology. The war effort also highlighted the strategic importance of ball bearings, leading to targeted efforts to protect and expand bearing manufacturing capabilities.

Post-war economic growth and industrialization further fueled the demand for ball bearings. The automotive industry, in particular, became a major consumer of bearings, with applications in engines, transmissions, wheel hubs, and various other components. The expansion of global trade and manufacturing also increased the need for reliable and efficient bearings in machinery, equipment, and transportation systems.

In the latter half of the 20th century, advancements in materials science, manufacturing, and computer technology continued to drive improvements in ball bearing design and performance. The development of ceramic ball bearings, which use ceramic materials instead of steel for the rolling elements, provided significant benefits in terms of reduced weight, increased hardness, and higher temperature resistance. These properties made ceramic ball bearings ideal for high-speed and high-temperature applications, such as in aerospace and precision machinery.

The advent of computer-aided design (CAD) and computer-aided manufacturing (CAM) technologies revolutionized the design and production of ball bearings. Engineers could now use sophisticated software to model and simulate bearing performance, optimizing designs for specific applications and operating conditions. Advanced manufacturing techniques, such as precision grinding and automated assembly, ensured higher quality and consistency in bearing production.

The rise of globalization and the growth of international supply chains further transformed the ball bearing industry. Leading bearing manufacturers established production facilities and distribution networks around the world, ensuring the availability of high-quality bearings to meet the needs of diverse markets and industries. The standardization of bearing sizes and specifications facilitated interoperability and compatibility across different applications and regions.

In recent decades, the focus on sustainability and energy efficiency has influenced the development of ball bearings. Manufacturers have sought to reduce the environmental impact of bearing production and operation through the use of eco-friendly materials, energy-efficient manufacturing processes, and improved lubrication systems. The development of low-friction and high-efficiency bearings has contributed to the overall energy savings in machinery and equipment, aligning with broader efforts to reduce energy consumption and carbon emissions.

Today, ball bearings are an integral component of countless devices and systems, from household appliances and office equipment to industrial machinery and transportation vehicles. Their versatility, reliability, and efficiency make them essential for reducing friction and enabling smooth rotational motion in a wide range of applications. The continued advancement of materials, design, and manufacturing technologies ensures that ball bearings will remain a critical element of modern engineering and innovation.

Chapter 50: The History of the Light Switch

The history of the light switch is a fascinating journey through technological innovation, electrical engineering, and the evolution of domestic life. The development of the light switch is intrinsically linked to the advent of electric lighting and the broader adoption of electricity in homes and businesses. This narrative spans more than a century, reflecting significant advancements in science, technology, and societal needs.

Before the invention of electric lighting, people relied on various sources of illumination such as oil lamps, gas lights, and candles. These methods, while functional, were often hazardous, inefficient, and required constant maintenance. The quest for safer and more efficient lighting solutions led to the exploration of electric light, a pursuit that culminated in Thomas Edison and Joseph Swan's development of the practical incandescent light bulb in the late 19th century. The invention of the light bulb was revolutionary, but it required a reliable and safe means of controlling the flow of electricity—enter the light switch.

The earliest forms of electrical switches were simple and rudimentary, often consisting of exposed contacts that had to be manually connected or disconnected to complete the circuit. These early switches were not only inconvenient but also posed significant safety risks, including electric shocks and short circuits. The need for a safer, more user-friendly solution was evident, and inventors set to work on developing better designs.

One of the first significant advancements in light switch technology was the toggle switch, invented by John Henry Holmes, a British engineer, in 1884. Holmes' design featured an enclosed mechanism that significantly reduced the risk of electric shock. The toggle switch used a spring-loaded lever to open or close the electrical circuit, providing a simple, reliable, and safe means of controlling electric lights. This design quickly gained popularity and laid the foundation for modern light switch technology.

Parallel to Holmes' work, other inventors and engineers were developing their own versions of the light switch. For instance, the push-button switch, which emerged in the late 19th and early 20th centuries, offered an alternative to the toggle switch. The push-button switch typically featured two buttons—one for turning the light on and the other for turning it off. This design was particularly popular in the early 20th century and can still be found in some vintage homes and buildings.

The early 20th century was a period of rapid electrification, particularly in the United States and Europe. The growing availability of electric power and the increasing adoption of electric lighting in homes and businesses created a substantial demand for reliable and safe light switches. Manufacturers began producing switches on a large scale, and standardization of electrical components became essential to ensure compatibility and safety.

The rotary switch was another important innovation in light switch design. Unlike the toggle and push-button switches, the rotary switch operated by turning a knob to open or close the circuit. This design was often used in conjunction with dimmer switches, allowing users to adjust the brightness of their lights. Rotary switches became popular in the mid-20th century and are still used today in various applications.

The mid-20th century also saw the introduction of the mercury switch, a novel design that utilized the conductive properties of mercury to open or close an electrical circuit. Mercury switches were particularly valued for their durability and reliability, as they contained no moving parts that could wear out or break. However, concerns about the environmental and health impacts of mercury led to a decline in their use over time.

As technology advanced, so too did the design and functionality of light switches. The latter half of the 20th century saw the development of more sophisticated switches, including those with integrated dimmers, timers, and motion sensors. Dimmer switches, which allow users to adjust the intensity of their lighting, became increasingly popular in the 1970s and 1980s. These switches use various technologies, such as rheostats and triacs, to modulate the voltage supplied to the light, enabling precise control over brightness and energy consumption.

The integration of electronic components into light switches also paved the way for programmable and remote-controlled switches. Programmable switches can be set to turn lights on or off at specific times, providing convenience and enhancing energy efficiency. Remote-controlled switches, often operated via infrared or radio frequency signals, offer the convenience of controlling lights from a distance, a feature particularly useful in large homes or commercial settings.

The turn of the 21st century brought about the era of smart technology, revolutionizing the way we interact with our home environments. Smart light switches, which can be controlled via smartphones, voice assistants, or automation systems, have become increasingly common. These switches are often part of broader smart home ecosystems, allowing for integration with other devices such as thermostats, security systems, and home entertainment systems. Smart switches offer a range of features, including remote control, scheduling, and integration with virtual assistants like Amazon Alexa, Google Assistant, and Apple's Siri.

One notable advancement in smart switch technology is the development of touch-sensitive and capacitive switches. These switches use the conductive properties of the human body to detect touch, eliminating the need for physical buttons or levers. Touch-sensitive switches provide a sleek, modern look and are often combined with LED indicators to provide visual feedback.

The evolution of light switch technology has also been influenced by changes in building codes and safety standards. Modern electrical codes mandate the use of grounding and proper insulation in switches to prevent electrical shocks and fires. Additionally, innovations such as ground fault circuit interrupters (GFCIs) and arc fault circuit interrupters (AFCIs) have enhanced the safety of electrical systems, including light switches, by detecting and interrupting potentially dangerous electrical faults.

Another important aspect of light switch evolution is the consideration of accessibility and universal design. Light switches are now designed to be easily operable by people with disabilities, incorporating features such as larger buttons, rocker switches, and voice control. This emphasis on accessibility ensures that everyone, regardless of physical ability, can safely and conveniently control their lighting.

Environmental sustainability has also become a key consideration in the design of light switches. Manufacturers are increasingly using eco-friendly materials and production processes to reduce the environmental impact of their products. Additionally, the development of energy-efficient lighting technologies, such as LED lights, has influenced the design of light switches to accommodate these new light sources and optimize energy usage.

Epilogue

As we come to the end of our journey through "The Untold History of Everyday Objects," it's clear that the items we often overlook hold fascinating stories and profound significance. We've explored the evolution of different everyday objects, each with its unique path of innovation and impact on our daily lives. These objects, in their simplicity and ubiquity, serve as silent witnesses to human progress, creativity, and resilience.

Reflecting on the toothbrush, the zipper, the light bulb, and many more, we see a common thread: the relentless human drive to solve problems and improve our world. Each object started as an idea, a spark of inspiration that led to experimentation, development, and eventually, widespread adoption. These inventions have not only made our lives more convenient but also catalyzed further innovations, creating a ripple effect across various fields.

Consider the sticky note, born from a failed adhesive experiment that turned into a ubiquitous office supply. Its story is a reminder that not all success comes from straightforward paths; sometimes, it emerges from unexpected twists and turns. The paperclip, a simple yet indispensable tool, teaches us that even the most modest invention can have a significant impact. The journey of the safety pin reveals how necessity truly is the mother of invention, driving solutions that become integral parts of our lives.

As we look around our homes, workplaces, and cities, we are surrounded by the fruits of countless inventors' labors. The mundane becomes extraordinary when we understand the stories behind these objects.

These stories also remind us of the power of perseverance. Many of these inventions faced initial skepticism, financial hurdles, and technical challenges. Yet, their creators persisted, fueled by a belief in their ideas and a vision for the future. Their determination not only brought their inventions to life but also paved the way for further advancements, showing us that innovation is a never-ending journey.

In our fast-paced, technology-driven world, it's easy to take for granted the everyday objects that simplify our lives. But as we've seen, each of these objects has a rich history, full of lessons and inspirations. They are more than mere tools; they are embodiments of human thought, effort, and imagination.

As we close this book, let's carry forward an appreciation for the ingenuity embedded in our daily lives. The next time you reach for a coffee mug, turn on a light switch, or use a safety pin, remember the stories and the people behind these objects. Let their histories inspire you to look at the world with curiosity and gratitude.

"The Untold History of Everyday Objects" is more than just a collection of histories; it's a celebration of human achievement and the spirit of innovation. It invites us to acknowledge the extraordinary in the ordinary and to recognize the ongoing legacy of inventors whose contributions continue to shape our world.

The End.